THE **AWAKENING** OF
HOPE

This book is good news. Jonathan Wilson-Hartgrove reports gatherings in homes and prisons and the inner city—all over the place. This is a magnificent report on lived theology, not just theological ideas and truths, but storied theology, the kind that we find in our Scriptures.

Eugene Peterson, translator of *The Message*

This is a superb and troubling book. *The Awakening of Hope* gives us the most complete statement to date of what the new monasticism is. To read it is to be rendered humble before the rugged vision that is being lived out here, and I, as a lay Christian, am deeply grateful.

Phyllis Tickle, author of *Emergence Christianity: What It Is, Where It Is Going, and Why It Matters*

If you believe that being Christian is adopting a counter-cultural lifestyle, marked by a deep sense of community, then this book is for you. It lets you know that you're not alone if you abandon an individualistic, consumeristic value system and commit to living in simple ways that are as ancient as the earliest days of the Church.

Tony Campolo, Eastern University

Jonathan Wilson-Hartgrove has written a brilliant catechism of hope for our desperate, grace-filled time.

James W. Douglass, author of *JFK and the Unspeakable*

Also by Jonathan Wilson-Hartgrove

Mirror to the Church
(Emmanuel M. Katongole with Jonathan Wilson-Hartgrove)

God's Economy

Common Prayer
(with Shane Claiborne and Enuma Okoro)

The Wisdom of Stability

New Monasticism

THE **AWAKENING** OF
HOPE

Why We Practice a Common Faith

JONATHAN WILSON-HARTGROVE

ZONDERVAN®

ZONDERVAN.com/
AUTHORTRACKER
follow your favorite authors

ZONDERVAN

The Awakening of Hope
Copyright © 2012 by Jonathan Wilson-Hartgrove

This title is also available as a Zondervan ebook. Visit www.zondervan.com/ebooks.

This title is also available in a Zondervan audio edition. Visit www.zondervan.fm.

Requests for information should be addressed to:

Zondervan, *Grand Rapids, Michigan* 49530

Library of Congress Cataloging-in-Publication Data

Wilson-Hartgrove, Jonathan, 1980 –
    The awakening of hope : why we practice a common faith / Jonathan Wilson-
    Hartgrove.
        p. cm.
        ISBN 978-0-310-29338-5
        1. Spiritual formation. 2. Christian life. 3. Christian communities. 4.
    Monasticism and religious orders. I. Title.
    BV4509.5.W525   2012
    269 – dc23   2012006775

Published in association with the literary agency of Daniel Literary Group, LLC, 1701 Kingsbury Drive, Suite 100, Nashville, TN 37215.

Cover design: Jay and Kristi Smith / Juicebox Designs
Cover illustration: Jay and Kristi Smith / Juicebox Designs
Interior illustration: iStockphoto®
Interior design: Beth Shagene
Editorial team: Carolyn McCready, Bob Hudson, Leigh Clouse,
Britta Eastburg, Alicia Sheppard, and Abbie Hudson

Printed in the United States of America

12 13 14 15 16 17 18 /DCI/ 21 20 19 18 17 16 15 14 13 12 11 10 9 8 7 6 5 4 3 2 1

For Marty

Contents

Foreword by Shane Claiborne

JONATHAN WILSON-HARTGROVE HAS CREATED A GIFT TO the church.

Over the past few decades, much of the energy of the Christian church has gone toward "evangelism"—but our evangelical fervor has come at a price. We have not spent as much energy on formation and discipleship. So we find ourselves in an age of shallow spirituality, where much of our Christianity is a mile wide and an inch deep.

We have focused on the beliefs rather than the practices of our faith. But doctrines are hard things to love. In Jesus we don't see just a presentation of ideas, but an invitation to join a movement that embodies God's good news. *The Awakening of Hope* is about that movement.

Over and over, studies have shown that belief does not equal changed lives. You can believe in the bodily resurrection of Jesus and still not live differently in light of it. You can believe the Scripture is the inerrant word of God and still not do what it says.

Too often we focus on the beliefs of the Christian faith without considering how those beliefs get fleshed out in real life and practice. In the end, Jesus, as part of his great commission, sent his own followers out into the world not just to make believers—but to make disciples.

The Awakening of Hope is a corrective to our belief-only Christianity. Jonathan reminds us of the holy habits that have marked Christians for centuries. He dusts off these classic spiritual disciplines and polishes them up for a new generation.

Without trivializing the essential beliefs and doctrines of our faith, Jonathan reminds us that our real challenge today is not just right-believing—but right living. He puts belief and practice back together again. After all, some folks think themselves into right living, and other folks live themselves into right thinking.

What's great about this project is that it doesn't just tell you what to do but tells you why Christians do the things they do. It is not a prescription for community but a description of what healthy community can look like. Jonathan tells you *why* Christians do these peculiar things—like fast from food and die instead of kill. And Jonathan offers a compelling invitation to join the millions of saints and wannabe saints throughout history in these practices of the faith.

And many of these practices are peculiar. They are marks of the holy counterculture that God has been forming for centuries. They invite you not to conform to the patterns of this world but to be transformed with a new imagination. Jonathan shows us vividly the inertia of the Gospel pulls us a different direction from the compelling pulls of our culture.

It is no coincidence that the word *disciple* shares the same root as the word *discipline.* No doubt many postmodern, post-Christian, post-evangelical, post-everything folks will cringe at the idea of discipline—but without it we end up with a pretty sloppy spirituality.

I remember reading about an interview with one of the social psychologists who pioneered the movement of "hands-off" parenting, insisting that our children do not need discipline. These scientists insisted children needed freedom, space to make their own decisions and mistakes. At the end of his life, one of the psychologists was asked what he had learned from years of experimentation. His response was, "It all looked good on paper. But what we learned was that we were creating a generation of brats."

In all our liberal inclusiveness and seeker-sensitivity, we must be careful not to create a generation of spiritual brats. Jonathan has helped us here—to recapture the disciplines that help us become better disciples. In this book and DVD study, Jonathan explores this question: What are the holy habits that turn ordinary people into saints?

And just like jogging or exercising at the gym, at first it is really hard to exercise our soul, but the more you do it the healthier you become. You start to feel yourself breathe better. You can feel the heart beat inside your chest and know you are alive.

So get ready to exercise. Here's a workout guide for your soul.

Introduction

SINCE THE CHRISTIAN MOVEMENT BEGAN TWO THOUSAND years ago, the mission of the church has been to communicate God's great story to a world that has been redeemed. When this story grabs hold of a person and turns their whole life around, we usually call it *conversion*. When God's story touches a deep need in society, giving rise to new ways of living, we call it *revival*.

This book is for people who have a hunch, whether you like the language of revival or not, that God is stirring a new movement in our world today. Call it what you will, if Jesus has grabbed you in a way that you know isn't just about you and your soul ... if God's vision of peace and justice burns in your bones ... if you've longed to see the love we were made for lived out in community—this book is for you.

This is a book for people who've tasted the hope of God's revival.

If we pay attention to history, revival has been important to every peace and justice movement America has known, from the abolitionist and women's suffrage movements of the nineteenth century to the civil rights movement of the 1960s.

When I walk downtown in the city where I live, I see the vestiges of revivals-gone-by in institutions with names like *Salvation Army* and *YMCA*, *Rescue Mission* and *Urban Ministries*. All of these organizations still *do* great things. But they don't do them with the same conviction as Salvation Army founder William Booth had when he said, "While women weep, as they do now, I'll fight; while children go hungry, as they do now, I'll fight; while men go to prison, in and out, in and out, as they do now, I'll fight; while there is a drunkard left, while there is a poor lost girl upon the streets, while there remains one dark soul without the light of God, I'll fight—I'll fight to the very end!"[1]

The mission of the church is always to connect God's story with society's deep need.

The mission of the church is also to keep telling God's story in a way that helps us remember why we do the things we do.

True revival is not the sort of thing you can plan and orchestrate on five successive weeknights with a guest preacher from out of town. Still, revival happens when hope grabs hold of us and won't let go. When justice begins to flow down like waters and righteousness like an ever-flowing stream, the river of faith swells its banks and you do what you can to hold on for the ride. You've been caught up into something bigger than yourself—something you can't explain. You whisper, "Thank you, thank you," as you go to bed at night. No one need remind you to say a prayer.

Revival is exhilarating and mysterious and awe-inspiring. It is a collective spiritual high. But if its power is to last—if the new life that the Spirit breathes is to make a lasting difference in our world—the experience of hope must find its place in a story that is true. As Peter, who testified at the first Pentecost, wrote, "Always be prepared ... to give the reason for the hope that you have" (1 Peter 3:15).

Hope has its reasons, for sure. Since its very beginnings, the Christian movement has passed these reasons on to all believers in basic teaching called *catechism*. Literally "to sound down," *catechism* has always been about a very embodied and engaged transmission of God's story from person-to-person, from one generation "down" to another. Traditional tools for this process are in a question-and-answer format. They are meant to serve as a framework for conversation, a springboard for storytelling.

While this book (and the DVD that goes with it) is not a conventional catechism, it aims to reengage this ancient practice for our own time. It tells the whole of God's story in response to "why" questions. Instead of saying what we believe and how we might apply that to our lives (as a typical sermon might), I've tried to focus on practices that inspire hope in our time and ask what convictions undergird a way of life that makes such witness possible. Each chapter moves from a picture of hope to the reasons that frame it within the Christian story.

Like all catechisms, this book is meant to start conversation. I hope the pictures of hope I've selected will remind you of others that you've seen and that those saints and communities will point beyond the convictions I've outlined to a deeper understanding of Scripture and the church's teaching.

For the sake of facilitating your conversation with friends, the study guide at the end of this book introduces the same teachings that the chapters cover in a more systematic fashion. I was glad to work with my friend Shane Claiborne on a six-session DVD that follows the central questions of this book. We hope that the book and DVD together present a new kind of catechism for our time. It's offered in hope that new communities of faithfulness will spring up all around as little groups gather in homes and community centers, on cell blocks and in class rooms to talk about the fire that's stirring in their bones.

No matter how dark things may seem in our world, fresh winds continue to stir new movements, reminding us that creation has been and is being redeemed. God is active, and the gospel has power to grab hold of our lives and our world with an undeniable force. We pay attention to the stirrings of revival because we always need signs of hope to point us toward God's kingdom. We always need fresh wind and fresh fire to push us forward.

But that is not all we need. As much as revival may serve to energize God's movement, we also need catechism to direct it. Just as a jet engine is useless—even dangerous—without sensitive controls to guide it, revival is a gift that we cannot receive and celebrate without the teaching that helps us to name what God is doing and where it is leading us. Without this wisdom, we easily burn out or rush on in the wrong direction.

The good news is that God has already given us all that we need to enjoy the life we were made for in Jesus Christ.

For every new sign of hope, there is ancient wisdom to help us interpret how a new thing can be rooted in God's old, old story. For every fresh wind, there is a rudder to lead us on toward the beloved community of God's kingdom here on earth as it is in heaven.

When the Spirit stirs to awaken us, there are reasons for our hope. We learn them not only to share with others, but also to help us see the revival that's happening where we are.

CHAPTER 1

Pictures of Hope

THEY TRICKLE IN BY TWOS AND THREES, SOMETIMES FROM across town, as often from across the country. They've caught the bus or they've caught a plane. They've driven eighteen hours straight, six people packed in a four-door sedan. One fellow hitchhiked for three days, sleeping under the stars on the flat tops of fast-food restaurants. He got here on little more than hope and a prayer.

They come from college campuses and from house churches, from a four-month backpacking trip and straight from the office (always with the apology, "Sorry I'm late"). A whole group comes from Norway, meeting an American missionary from Amsterdam en route. They realize they're going to the same place and show up together. A young woman on her way out of town tells her friend about where she's going, and the friend decides she'd like to come along for the ride. Surely their hosts won't mind. They knit hats in the passenger's seat to offer as housewarming gifts.

Their faces are young and bright, eyes ablaze with ideals they would like to live out. They are sometimes middle-aged and sober, holding on to hope by a thread. A few are marked by wrinkles that grow deeper when they smile. Sometimes a face tells the whole story. But not always. One good-looking young man is all smiles, eager to meet new people and able to make everyone feel comfortable. To look at him, you'd never know the loneliness he'll later describe to me—the hole in his heart that's driving his cocaine addiction.

They come sleepy, hungry, road weary, and eager. They come looking for something. Some find fellow travelers— people from their own city, even, whom they didn't know before. Some find a home. They just pick up and move, ready to leave everything for something that's grabbed them, some- thing that won't let go. A handful have found a special con- nection, traded contact information, and called two years later to say they're getting married. I'm not sure what some people leave with, but you can tell by the way they say "Thank you" that it means something to them. Whatever they've found, they take it home with them. And life is new.

They come for a taste of Christian community. Someone told them at some point in their life that they had to go to school to master reading and writing, to expand their minds in the liberal arts, to learn to practice business or law, ministry or medicine. They've all been to school before. But they come here because they want more. They want to learn how to live. They have a hunch that Jesus should be their guide. Having set out to follow him, they've found their way to community.

Sometimes they get lost and have to stop to ask for direc- tions. They can tell from the way the guy at the corner store looks at them that they're not supposed to be here. The kid on the corner just stares, so they ask again. Even in their own hometowns, this is sometimes their first afternoon on this side of the highway, this side of the tracks. Whether they've traveled two thousand miles or two, they've leapt across a wall. Everyone's adrenaline is up. Something is about to happen.

For the past decade, I have walked alongside these pilgrims, meeting them at the place where their personal journey intersects with the story of a Christian community that embodies the hope they seek. As diverse and unpredictable as their stories may be, it is this moment of recognition that unites them. In the lived witness of people who have given their lives to the way of Jesus, these diverse souls glimpse an authenticity their hearts long for. Far from a utopia, these messy gatherings of broken people inspire hope not because they are perfect, but because they point to the possibility that another way is possible. Indeed, something *is* happening.

Signs That Grab Our Hearts

Sixteen hundred years ago in northern Egypt, thousands of pilgrims left their homes and work in the city to go out into the desert. Each with their own story, they went seeking a word from hermits who had established small monastic communities and devoted themselves to prayer. The church at that time was embroiled in doctrinal and political struggles, its leadership divided and its faithful often at odds with one another. If the bishops of the fourth century had blogged, the buzz would have been about contested elections, accusations of corruption, and theological disputes about Christology. They were arguing about things that mattered, of course. But they were also overlooking some of the most important things happening nearby.

Something was happening out in the desert that captivated the hearts of everyday people in the fourth century. Early Christian monasticism created a space where those who cared about the truth of the gospel could ask how it shaped their daily life. Across the distance of time, we can look back and see how those lives were united in a movement that changed both the church and the world. Framed by the story of God's movement in human history, they stand out as a picture of hope.

We too live in a time when Christians are fragmented, our leadership embroiled in controversy and our congregations at odds. Much of what amounts to news in the church today is accusations of scandal and debates about homosexuality and atonement theories. To folks outside the church, faith is often perceived as an ugly fight about something that seems to make very little real difference in how people live. What passes for religious news is seldom good news. But people are hungry for good news they can enjoy in the places where they live. Most of them are looking for a picture of hope.

This is what I hear from the pilgrims who keep coming to new monastic communities in the forgotten inner cities and overlooked farmlands of North America. They need more than an explanation of the world that makes sense, more than an experience that assures them God is in his heaven and we're going to be all right. They want to see what hope looks like. They ache for a place on earth where all that they believe can get fleshed out—where faith can put on blue jeans and go to work. Our conversations inevitably turn toward a faith that is not "mine" but "ours," a common vision connecting us to an extended family stretching beyond the borders of our homelands and social networks. Together we see how much we need the way of life that Jesus shows us. We need the hope that comes from glimpsing what real life can look like here and now.

Before anyone invited them, these pilgrims came. They came because they heard a story about black folks and white folks sitting down to dinner together in the American South twenty years before the civil rights movement. They came because they met Central American refugees who fled their homes seeking political asylum in the 1980s and found sanctuary in some Christian communities willing to offer hospitality despite their own government's insistence that such welcome was illegal. They came because they got interested in the Catholic peace movement; when they followed the activists home from prison, they found a community. They came because they heard an interview or read a book about a way of life that seemed to make sense. They came to see if the story that captivated their hearts was for real.

As much as I share the longings of these pilgrims, I confess to being mystified by their presence. Every time I meet a new group I ask myself again, "Where did these people come from?" This persistent question has kept me thinking about those Egyptian monks in the fourth century and their visitors, about the colossal shift the church faced 1600 years ago and the changes swirling about us today. If I can draw any sort of conclusion from my reflections on these matters, it is this:

the reality of God's new order seems stubbornly insistent on its own terms. That is, God's new thing—both then and now—breaks into the world as we know it, disrupts the status quo, disturbs the peace that is no peace, and reminds us that another world is possible here and now.

God's movement is, in short, an interruption. For those who walk in darkness, it is a flash of light. It catches the eye, you might say. Like a picture of hope.

God and the Big Questions

God always makes the first move. To know the God of the Bible is to trust the God who created everything out of nothing, not because more was needed to somehow complete the circle, but simply because it pleased God. There's nothing necessary about our existence, just as there's nothing we can do to force God's movement in the world. God always makes the first move. Faithful action, then, is always a response.

So, if you're a bishop of the church in the turmoil of the fourth century, there's nothing you can do to guarantee the future of the church. And if you're a passionate, thoughtful person at the beginning of the twenty-first century, eager to sort out the big questions about God and life, there's nowhere you can go to start figuring everything out for sure. However strong our desire, however fervent our initiative, it's never enough. God always makes the first move. The Spirit blows where it will. When it does, it often blows our minds.

But after you've been knocked off your feet—after the Spirit has hovered over the chaos of your life and hurled you forward into a future beyond the limits of your vision—the questions are still there. God's interruption doesn't answer our questions. It doesn't erase them either. It leaves us, rather, with a photo album full of pictures of hope.

This is where theology begins. An album full of pictures before us, we begin to sort out the reasons for the hope that has been stirred up within us. "Keep asking the big questions," God whispers. But don't start with your own frustrations and disappointment. Don't start where you started before, with your own longings and dreams. Start with the places where hope emerged. Start with Israel in Egypt, with shepherds near Bethlehem, with people breaking bread in Emmaus, with monks in the desert, with little communities off the radar where something new is stirring. Start here, and ask, "What's going on?" Ask where God is moving and receive that first move as an invitation to you, an invitation to respond. All the living and thinking, acting and reflecting that follows is what makes for a faithful life.

The contemporary movement in North American Christianity sometimes called "the new monasticism" is one response. Like the tradition that started in fourth-century Egypt, ours is a minority movement, often found on the fringes of official denominations and local congregations. If we have been known for any one thing, it is an emphasis on putting faith into practice. With small groups of people who've had the time and freedom to do so, we've tried to devote our whole lives to living out the way of Jesus as outlined in the Sermon on the Mount. We do this with full awareness that Jesus' way of living is an interruption not only to the ways of the world around us, but also to our own ways of thinking and living.

Our emphasis on the "right-living" of faith—*orthopraxis*—is, no doubt, something of a reaction against a perceived over-emphasis on *orthodoxy*, the "right-teaching" of faith. "Don't tell me what you believe," some say, "show me how you live." (I must admit, I've said it myself.) While at a gut level this response may be the right instinct in a situation where the affirmation of doctrine has not led to consistent and faithful reflection on it, pitting doctrine against practice is a dead end because it denies the essential connection between God's movement and our response.

Central Christian doctrines describe God's action. Incarnation, for example, is the teaching that God became human in Jesus so that humanity might have a way to become like God. This is infinitely practical. God does not take on flesh and move into the neighborhood without changing the place. Believing that this is true changes the pattern of our everyday lives. Our efforts to live faithfully always include action and reflection.

In short, pictures of hope point us toward God and the Big Questions.

Good living entails good reflection. Having been interrupted by Jesus, we carry our questions with us. They become part of our relationship with the living God, evoked by the pictures of hope that capture our imagination. As a people who are well trained in adapting to the latest technology, it is not surprising that we would first ask *how*? How do we resist the power of consumerism? How do we honor and care for creation? How do we live together in a world where families and communities are falling apart? If Jesus really meant all that stuff he said, *How should we live our lives?*

How is an important question that trains our eyes to pay attention to the practicalities of a life lived with God and other people in communion. But if *how* is the question of our age, the concern at the forefront of our minds, then God's interruption of our status quo also presents a new question —a question that's equally practical and maybe even more radical. That question is, *why?*

Why would people choose to eat together in a time when individual freedom and consumer choice are a premium for most Americans?

Why would people who are financially independent decide to share money and financial decisions with others?

Why would someone risk their life by going into a war zone unarmed to be with their nation's enemies?

This is a book about *why*.

Why do people who follow Jesus do the things we do?

Dorothy Day, one of the founders of the Catholic Worker Movement, used to say that we ought to live in such a way that our lives wouldn't make sense if the gospel were not true. Communities that live according to Day's advice exist as interruptions in society, experiments conducted to remind us that the way things are is not the way things have to be. If folks have any sense that all is not right in the world, these interruptions can present a picture of hope. People will come to see—they'll come, if nothing else, to see if it's all just a sham. But if seeing is believing—if the reality on the ground really does point to something beyond the values and norms of the American way—then the same people will ask *why?*

Behind the practice that catches the eye there is a conviction, a gospel that makes sense of a peculiar way of living. Surrounding every picture of hope, there is a frame. *Wherever it is real, hope has its reasons.*

The traditional name for this frame is "doctrine." This logic of hope is the teaching of God's people, growing out of Scripture and always aimed at helping people live the Bible's story in the present—that is, in conversation with all that's happening in the world around us. At its best, this teaching flourishes in those spaces where God's Spirit is at work and among people who are being transformed by the remaking power of participation in God's beloved community. While it may be informed by academic study and critical reflection, true doctrine—orthodoxy—is the fruit of faithful living with God and other people.

For most of Christian history, a great deal of this teaching has arisen from the monastic communities that trace their roots to fourth century Egypt. Monastic historian Columba Stewart has called these communities "laboratories of Christian spirituality," noting that a disproportionate number of the church's most influential teachers in the East and West have done their living and reflecting in monasteries.[2] I suspect this has something to do with the fact that monastics are the people who've been given the freedom to devote most of their energy toward living the way of Jesus. What intrigues me is how many of their works are written as responses to questions. Might some of these have come from the pilgrims who came looking for a picture of hope? Did monasteries teach doctrine partly because so many people came to them asking *why*?

St. Augustine said that the church exists as a people "on the way," which is another way of saying that we're all pilgrims. Together with my family, I've made a promise of stability to the Rutba House community in Durham, North Carolina. We are on our way in this particular place. But the pilgrims who come and go through our doors remind me of this persistent *why* that has driven theological reflection throughout human history. It's a question we all ask eventually, whether it's on your fortieth birthday, or on the day you get deployed, or on the drive to see the doctor after she's called to say, "The tests came back; they don't look good." It's a question we ask because life has a way of pushing us right to the edge of what we know, then leaving us there to think about it, even if only for a second.

Some of us get there sooner than others. For one in every thousand or so, the question burns so bright that he has to hit the road, even though he doesn't own a car or have the money to catch a bus. He trusts providence and leans on the generosity of truckers, borrowing a dry rooftop from the Burger King, where he can lay flat and stare up at the stars. Folks like him don't get to sleep easy, but they have lots to think about, and they like to look up on a wide open sky. When someone like me answers their knock at the door, a sky full of cosmic questions pours across my life for a few days, and I'm reminded of the mystery that both compels and sustains this fragile life of faith. We hold hope between us with delicate hands.

On my best days, I thank the good Lord for people like that, for someone who looks at the way we're living and asks with their whole being, "Why?" After they're gone, I do the things I'm used to doing, but with new eyes. Somehow, I think to myself, it's not quite the same when you see it in this light. *Why* reshapes the *what*—makes you reconsider the *how*, even. It's hard to put into words, but I remember that I've had this sense before. It was the last time someone came asking *why?* I don't have an answer typed out, ready to hand to the next pilgrim who comes along, but I'm the sort of seeker who finds his way with a string of words, so I promise myself I'll sit with the question.

CHAPTER 2

Why We Eat Together

IT'S FIVE O'CLOCK ON A SUNDAY AFTERNOON IN SAN FRAN-cisco's Mission District, and I'm stretched out on the grass in a backyard garden, catching up with friends while we take in the sun that you can never quite get enough of in Northern California. The lemons on the tree against the back fence are ripe, ready to be enjoyed. Their skins shine with the setting sun, aglow like the faces of folks who are gathering to worship after a day of sweet rest. This is the Church of the Sojourners, a community of Christians who live together in four large houses seven days a week and worship with friends and neighbors on Sunday evenings.

I've spent the whole weekend here as a guest of the community, and so I have learned a bit about the rules of the house. On this, their Sabbath day, there is no talking before lunch. They rose on their own schedules, early or late, and ate breakfast quietly in their kitchens. Kids went off on scheduled outings with one parent or the other, and everyone else settled into a morning of quiet. Some sat in the garden, where we are now, reading Scripture or meditating in silence. Others stayed in their rooms or went out on walks.

I sat at a desk with pen in hand, trying to pay attention. The world did not magically stop spinning around me. Some neighborhood kids were playing with firecrackers, chattering to one another before the expectant hush in which a sizzle preceded the inevitable blast, always followed by cheers. The clamor never stopped, but I heard the firecracker—not just the noise, but the explosion itself, ripping paper and air and the tension in young boys' souls. I wondered what irruptions I missed this week because, however loud, their interruption was overwhelmed by the din of constant motion and ceaseless sound. Here in the midst of the turning world, a still point.

I came to lunch with the expectancy of a kid who had just lit a firecracker, not sure what I might find, but with my ears open, alert. One conversation led to another until I landed here in this garden, breathing deep and enjoying good company. Another still point. I notice the lemons and, for a moment, see the life that is pulsing beneath their skin, ready to burst out. Someone here will eat that flesh, feel its fresh tartness on their tongue before returning its skin to the compost pile. I'm sitting in the midst of a dance, energized by soil and sun and sustained by the love that moves the stars. I hear music in the air.

Dale is playing a guitar, leading others into the garden. They join their voices in song as we form a circle across two backyards, the fence between them removed to make room for gatherings like this. Some fifty people stand facing one another, our singing finished with the song still hanging in the air between us. Debbie lifts a loaf of bread above her head. Tearing it in two, she says, "This is my body, broken for you."

Each half of the loaf makes its way around the circle, one person taking a piece and holding it in front of the next to say, "The body of Christ, broken for you." Receiving my piece, I eat it, then break off another to offer the person on my left.

After the halves of bread have made their way around the circle, Mike invites everyone into the house where he says our communion will continue with supper. A buffet is laid out on the counter, prepared by those who didn't rest in the garden but got to work in the kitchen after lunch. We pick from the bounty and proceed to find some place to eat, sitting or standing, like at the family reunions I grew up going to in the South. With every chair at the table filled, people spill over into the living room, balancing plates on their knees and talking with their mouths full. This family speaks Spanish and English, so I do my best to stumble through some conversations in a language not my own. A community that has kept silence bursts into conversation.

Above the clamor of the crowd, someone shouts a reminder to take our dirty plates to the dish team at the kitchen sink. Soon the guitars begin again, and we are singing. This is when I realize that we're in the midst of a worship service, only to recall that I am the guest preacher. I slip into the guest room to grab my Bible and notes. In the midst of a meal, preaching feels more conversational than it does when I stand behind a pulpit in an august sanctuary to proclaim a word from the Lord. When I am finished here, folks talk back. They reflect out loud on the good news they've heard and what they imagine it might mean to trust it in the coming week. The Bible and the preacher have become conversation partners, and we continue talking to each other.

Someone celebrates little Alexina, who was kind to her brother this week. Another thanks Terri for being a shoulder to lean on Tuesday night after a hard day at work and a string of bad luck. Little things, you might say, if you weren't there to see Alexina smile. But in that moment you see that she knows she is loved. You think of all the anxiety that works itself out in fear and violence because someone doesn't know that one thing, and you realize that nothing in all the world is more important than these little things. By little and by little, we are being saved.

Amid affirmations, some folks confess. One woman is sorry for her short temper. Another, her eyes heavy, says she's struggling with depression. Could we pray for her? A man in his sixties says his recovery isn't easy. He needs help. There is a silence—a still point—in which we wait. Then Debbie lifts a cup above her head and says, "This is the blood of my new covenant, poured out for you and for many for the forgiveness of sins. Do this as often as you drink it in remembrance of me."

The cup is passed from one person to the next, and we drink. It's dark outside, but no one seems to be in a hurry to disperse. Our eating has been about more than filling our bellies. We depart with a blessing, repeated on the lips of a dozen faces, pressed close to mine in an embrace: "The peace of Christ."

What happens on a Sunday evening at Church of the Sojourners is a snapshot of what God's people have been doing for centuries when we gather. We eat together. At the very beginning of our story, God plants a garden full of fruit bearing trees and invites us to come and eat. When God comes to Abraham and Sarah as three visitors, they all sit down and have a meal together. In the book of Acts, which records the earliest days of the church, we read that the sisters and brothers "devoted themselves to the apostles' teaching and to fellowship, *to the breaking of bread* and to prayer" (2:42). One of the main images Jesus uses for heaven is a wedding banquet —a huge dinner party—where all God's people kick back and enjoy a feast. Eating together, it seems, is what we are made for.

It's no accident that the Lord's Supper—or Eucharist —has been the centerpiece of Christian worship from the church's earliest days. To remind us of what God's love looks like in the world, Jesus gave us a meal—bread to be his body and wine as his life-blood, poured out for friends and enemies alike. Throughout the past two thousand years of church history, this meal has scandalized the status quo, bringing Jews and Gentiles, slaves and slave-owners, citizens and undocumented neighbors together at the same table. This revolutionary meal inspired black and white people across the American South to sit down at segregated lunch counters in 1960, insisting that they should be served together because they were equal in the eyes of the Lord. The white citizens who spat in their faces and put cigarettes out on their heads knew that it's no small thing for people to eat together.

If we want to understand what it means to join God's movement in the world today, there's no better place to begin than by asking why God's people eat together. It is, after all, a peculiar commitment in a time when even nuclear families rarely sit down to a common meal. As participants in a consumer culture, we bounce between ads that appeal to our personal appetites and diets that promise a healthier version of "me" if I stick to an individualized eating plan. We're used to grabbing fast food when we're in a hurry, fine foods when we can afford them, lite foods when we want to be healthy, and cheap food when we're broke. But whatever our preference, food choices are almost always about "me," not "we." We eat as individual consumers, not members of a body.

Subtle as it might seem at first, eating together is an interruption to business as usual—a constant reminder that God's movement goes against the grain of the status quo, calling us ever deeper into a new reality beyond the available options of this world's systems. Whether it happens in a backyard garden at a community house in San Francisco, in a fellowship hall on the plains, or at a kneeling rail in a cathedral, when God's people eat together we connect with the very foundations of our story.

Here we remember who we were made to be.

As creatures in communion, we learn the habits that make it possible to know what it means to say Jesus Christ is Lord.

Learning Who We Are at the Table

It's Tuesday night and my wife and I are on as cooks for our neighborhood potluck meal. We're making lasagna for thirty, so I start by chopping veggies and sautéing them in oil, savoring the smell of onions, sweet peppers, and mushrooms mixing together at 300 degrees. I can't begin to cook without thinking of those who will eat: Tom is deathly allergic to olives, so I pour canola oil into the pan; Sarah, Dan, and Matt are vegetarian, so I replace the traditional beef with tofu. If I get it right, even the carnivores will go for this lasagna, making everyone happy. All of these friends will be with us when we eat, but they are here even now as we prepare the food. Our life is tied up with theirs whether I remember them or not. But I better not forget, or I'll hear about it in two hours.

This meal depends on still others, though, many of whom thought of us long before we thought of them. We live in a city where natural-gas lines run beneath our streets, connecting house to house and street to street, all the way back to the supply. There, people I've never met have mastered science I don't understand to extract gas from beneath the earth, contain it for storage, and deliver it in just the right amount to the front right burner on my stove. They were even kind enough to add the scent of rotten eggs to the odorless gas so that when my pilot light goes out because of a draft from the front door I smell the leak before it kills my family. Whoever thought of that has saved our lives on more than one occasion. Our life depends on others whether we think of them or not.

What is more, it's winter here in North Carolina, and though we sometimes have kale and chard in our garden through January, the onions and mushrooms and red bell peppers I am chopping now came to us by way of our weekly shopping trip to the local grocery store. The store is less than a mile from our house, but these veggies racked up frequent flyer miles before they ever made it to the produce shelf. I have listened to stories of cucumber farmers here in North Carolina, and I have marched with migrant farm workers from Florida to ask their employers to pay a penny more per pound of produce, but the truth is I'm not sure where these particular vegetables came from or how many hands worked long hours for little pay to bring them to my kitchen. What I do know is that a meal for thirty, "homemade" in my kitchen, connects me to countless other people and places, animals and plants.

We are, no doubt, knit together in the food and energy systems that we have crafted through modern technology. But our connections go deeper—all the way down to the dirt, in fact—when we take time to pay attention to the basic necessities of life. This meal is not possible without the gift of good soil. In the Bible's account of creation, we read that God formed the first human from the humus of the ground, then breathed the breath of life into him. Life is a mystery, and we are, each of us, always more than dirt. But Genesis preserves a profound truth in this account that insists our lives depend on dirt. Indeed, the rich and complex universe that makes up soil may reveal the mystery of our being more clearly than the movement of God's breath, the other basic element in this story. Who, after all, can see a breath? But the dirt is always with us.

Still, most of us spend precious little time paying attention to soil. Five hundred years ago, at the dawn of the modern world, Leonardo da Vinci commented that "we know more about the movement of celestial bodies than we do about the soil underfoot." While this was true then, even for people who found meaning in the stars of the heavens, it would be equally honest to say that most of us today know more about our favorite movie stars than we do about the ground beneath us. In the rush of modern life, it is easy to forget that our primary vocation as human beings is to "till the earth and care for it." It's right there in the Bible, of course, but nothing brings this truth home like paying attention to the food we eat.

Attention, however, is not a habit we cultivate in modern life, even less in eating. Distraction is the fuel of our consumer culture, propelling us constantly forward to the next thing we are told we need. Eating is our most basic form of consumption. We really do need to eat, even if not as often and as much as most of us do. But to eat without attention is to reduce eating to the consumption of products. It is to believe in practice what farmer-poet Wendell Berry has called "the idea that money brings forth food."[3]

While a constant stream of ads for new food products may serve to convince us that there is an endless supply, demand is not the only factor determining the availability of food. Ultimately, food depends on good soil. But an economy that has not attended to its ecology can only understand soil as an externality—a part of the environment that is somehow out there, apart from the closed system in which people buy and sell products based on supply and self-interest. The trouble is that while soil doesn't fit into most economic equations, our life still depends on it. Working within this contradiction, industrial farmers are taught to kill soil with pesticides so they might then save it with fertilizers, echoing the peculiar logic of the US Army officer in Vietnam who famously said, "It became necessary to destroy the town to save it."

This rhetoric of total war rings in stark contrast to the language Scripture uses to introduce us to our origins in soil. This is why eating well is so important to our faith. When we stop to pay attention to food, we engage in nonviolent direct action against a culture of perpetual war that teaches us to fear anything we cannot control. Trained in the habits of a competitive marketplace, we are constantly tempted to think that our job is to provide for ourselves and our families over and against the enemies that threaten our existence, not the least of which is nature. Our seemingly innate desire to "climb the ladder" is, by definition, a longing to put the soil beneath us and conquer that enemy once and for all. But attending to food teaches us to love our enemy, to learn that our very existence depends on a new relationship of mutual care.

"Unless a seed falls into the ground and dies, it cannot bear fruit," Jesus says (see John 12:24, paraphrase). This process depends on the soil every bit as much as it requires the seed's submission to the humus—the virtue we traditionally call "humility." Jesus teaches humility because he knows we are bound to humus in ways we have not begun to comprehend. He gives himself to us as food so we might learn from soil something of what it means to be human.

In his book *Out of the Earth*, soil conservationist Daniel Hillel describes how dirt is "a rich mix of mineral particles, organic matter, gases, and nutrients which, when infused with vital water, constitutes a fertile substrate for the initiation and maintenance of life. The soil," he says, "is thus a self-regulating biological factory, utilizing its own materials, water, and energy from the sun."[4] Quite apart from human ingenuity, soil offers us the gift of a life that is sustainable, honoring the needs of all its members and keeping a rhythm that works for the whole. To know the soil as our source is to learn its wisdom and to honor its gift. When we remember that we came from dust and are returning to it, we see in daily life why *ecology* and *economy* share the same root in the Greek word for "home." We are never at home in the gift of God's creation until we reconcile our economic activity to the soil that is the basis of every ecosystem. We cannot eat well without learning the sort of membership that is manifest in the mystery of soil.

We are, each of us, benefactors of the soil. We eat together to remember this.

As I cover the lasagnas and carry them to another house where our community potluck is about to begin, I know there are easier, more efficient ways to get the calories I need at dinner time. Just a short drive from here, there's a nice little Italian restaurant where my family could enjoy dinner without even having to wash the dishes. Though not as tasty, the wholesale store has frozen lasagnas that cost less than these I've just finished making. But we've gone to the trouble to make this particular dinner for roughly the same reason we make an effort to eat with these particular people—because it seems more in keeping with the sort of community we are made for, even if it costs more time and money, even if it forces us to deal with people we'd sometimes rather avoid. One of the things we learn to name by eating together is that we are creatures, inextricably connected in a member-ship called creation. To deny that connection in practice is to reject the gift of life and to march, however slowly or blindly, toward our collective death.

When we see one another across the table, earth creatures who are sustained by the gifts of soil and one another, our eyes are sometimes opened to the potential of a peace that is beyond our making. In the story about the disciples who met Jesus on the road to Emmaus, Luke says they knew him "in the breaking of the bread." Knowing him, we know who we were made to be, even if only in glimpses. We eat together to remember the connections that sustain us, the membership that makes us who we are.

Eating Toward Communion

Before the Bible's story about God breathing life into the stuff of soil, Genesis gives another account of creation that culmi-nates in a quotation with peculiar grammar: "Let us make human beings in our image, in our likeness," God says. Then the narrator reports, "... so God created human beings in his own image, in the image of God he created them; male and female he created them" (1:26–27 TNIV). The odd wording of this passage fascinated early Christian teachers, prompting them to explore what it means for the one true God to speak to God's selves in the first person plural while being referred to in the third person singular, all within two verses of Holy Scripture. The doctrine of the Trinity emerged from close attention to this text and many others, giving the church language to express a deep mystery—namely, that God is always both three persons and one essence. What is more, humanity is created in the image of this God. Our unity, however basic it may be to our very essence, is always present to us in the plurality of community.

If the soil that is our common source reminds us we are creatures, then God's breath points us back to this first creation account, rooting our life together in the very life of God. To be human is to be both tied up in a membership with all of creation and at the same time knit together with other human beings in the image of God. If our eating together serves to remind us of the connections that tie us to soil, it should also point us toward our source (and end) in the Trinitarian God.

But just as we are in the habit of eating without attention to soil, we are also well practiced in eating apart from true life in God. Writing to the Christians at Corinth in first-century Greece, the apostle Paul said, "I hear that when you come together as a church, there are divisions among you.... When you come together, it is not the Lord's Supper you eat, for as you eat, some of you go ahead with your own private suppers. As a result, one person remains hungry and another gets drunk" (1 Corinthians 11:18, 21). What was true in the first century is amplified by globalization. One Sunday morning several years ago, I prayed with Christians in the Dominican Republic, begging for daily bread beside a river that had dried up and left fields barren. The next Sunday I was in a worship service in the US where the bulletin advertised a workshop to learn biblical principles for losing weight. The consequences of our eating poorly are not just unhealthy bodies, but a body politic in severe distress.

While this connection between physical and social health is important, Paul is focused on a more basic connection between our relationships with one another and our relationship with God. The fragmentation of a social system where some have too much while others have too little is not just a social problem or a justice issue for Paul. It is, rather, a denial of the Lord's Supper—a refusal of God's invitation in Jesus for us to eat the bread that satisfies and become the body that does not merely sustain life, but *is* life for the world. To eat in the isolation of social division is to eat toward death (however long our eating poorly may sustain us). But we are invited to eat well when we eat *together* at God's table. Here we join the feast that will last forever by becoming part of a body that lays itself down in love for one another.

In the communion that makes space for a dinner meal, back at the Church of the Sojourners, I find my way to a corner where a guy named Rick has a plate propped on his knee. I met Rick earlier and learned a bit about his life of organized crime back in New York City and a drug addiction that left him penniless on the West Coast.

"So Rick," I ask, "how'd you come to be part of this group?"

He smiles in the midst of chewing, then wipes his chin with the back of his hand to make sure nothing fell out. "I guess it was Jack," Rick says. "He loved me. Made me believe God could love me too. I've been here ever since."

For Christians, Jesus is "the image of the invisible God" who took on flesh and lived among us so that we could see, in the language of John's gospel, the *logos* lived out in the real world. This logic of the universe—the wisdom by which the whole world was made—is the knowledge of a Creator whose "thoughts are above our thoughts." We cannot comprehend the Trinity in whose image we are made. But we know Trinity looks like love because we have seen Jesus' way of living in the world—we know it because we've received the bread of life and passed it to our neighbor, "the body of Christ, broken for you." We begin to know what it means that God loves us when we are captivated by the love of a communion that draws us ever further into community.

"To be reconciled to one another is to be able to gather around a table with each other without shame, celebrating the gifts to each other that we are," writes contemporary theologian Norman Wirzba in his book *Food and Faith*. "It is to commit to an economy and politics in which the care of each other is our all-consuming desire."[5] When Christians eat together, we eat toward this vision. We need not be sentimental—this reconciling love is never fully realized in our fellowship. That it's not is an agonizing reality, not only because we want our ideals to line up with reality, but because we know we cannot have real life apart from our Lord's Supper. If division among us is a denial of this gift, then we have no hope apart from life together with friends and enemies at God's table. These concerns raise questions beyond our reasons for eating together.

Yet, even as we turn to those questions, we know that we eat together because we are sustained by a gift beyond us—that we receive what has been given so we can become what we were made to be. Because you've eaten with Rick, you know something about the love that saves and sustains you. Because he ate and lived with Jack, he knows something about the love of Jesus. Because you've each glimpsed the love of Jesus in your own way, you have seen the love of the Father, a love that is ever-flowing between Father, Son, and Holy Spirit, pulsing as the life-blood that sustains all creation.

You may not see it all the time, but every once in a while there is a still point when you're passing the asparagus and laughing at a bad joke. You look up from your plate and you see the image of God. And you know this is why we eat together.

CHAPTER 3

Why We Fast

ON A 260-ACRE COMMUNITY FARM OUTSIDE OF ATHENS, Georgia, Don and Carolyn Mosley live with about two dozen year-round staff and seasonal volunteers and a similar number of refugees from around the world. Their work is to keep the farm, help refugees prepare for life in the US, host over a thousand guests a year, serve as a bridge between American society and crises around the world, and pursue the kingdom of God with every fiber of their being. Since beginning this work in 1979, they have hosted nearly four thousand refugees from some three dozen countries. The world has come to them over the past three decades, and they have followed the stories of refugee friends back to peacemaking and development efforts in Central America, the Middle East, Southern Sudan, and North Korea. If you hang around and listen, they have stories to tell.

But coming down the gravel drive, through the woods and past the little houses that Don and Carolyn built with other Jubilee Partners and volunteer help, it doesn't appear that anything dramatic is happening here. People are growing much of their own food in a simple garden, milking a cow for their milk and butter. Others are busy doing maintenance work on buildings, filling out paperwork at desks, preparing meals in the large dining hall, or ferrying sick refugees to and from the doctor. Their income comes mostly from the donations of thousands of friends around the world, and they take pride in stretching every dollar as far as they can. Each partner gets a weekly allowance for personal expenses. "It used to be ten dollars a week," one of the partners tells me, "but we upped it to fifteen a few years ago."

It's a simple life, you might say—the sort of existence that hippies romanticized and back-to-the-land advocates hold out as an ideal today. But the Mosleys are no hippies, and they certainly haven't dropped out of the world of international affairs to focus solely on the local. The ambitious son of a Texas millionaire, Don joined the Peace Corps in the early 1960s to try to help make a difference in the world. After serving for two years in Malaysia and then, with Carolyn, as Peace Corps staff in South Korea, he might have come home to run the family business with a global perspective. He might have made a career in politics. Instead, he signed on to join God's movement for fifteen dollars a week.

Don is only one person, Jubilee Partners only one Christian community. But their existence is a reminder of communities and movements throughout Christian history that have given up good things for the sake of God's kingdom. While the monks and friars, priests and radicals who have embraced voluntary poverty have always been a minority among God's people, their witness highlights the practice of fasting, which has been common to all believers.

In his most famous sermon, Jesus' instructions about fasting come immediately after his introduction of the "Our Father" prayer, suggesting that the former should be as common as the latter. Before Jesus began his public ministry, the gospels record that he fasted for forty days in the wilderness. In the early church, if anyone in the fellowship was hungry, it was common practice for the whole community to go without until they could supply their brother or sister's need. As early as the fourth century, Christians began observing Lent —a season of fasting and repentance—in preparation for the Easter feast. Some restaurants still feature fish on Fridays, a vestige of a time not so long ago when Christians wouldn't enjoy a steak on the day that Jesus died.

Even so, the denial of something as basic as food can seem strange, especially if one of the most important things we do is eat together. If eating is so important—if it reveals to us both our identity as creatures in a membership and our destiny as participants in the life of God—why would we ever choose not to eat? For that matter, if the connections we witness in soil lead us to see our world as God's good gift (and not a prison from which we must escape), why would we deny ourselves any good thing? Why live on fifteen dollars a week when you could enjoy (and share) the abundance of a sizable inheritance?

For Don, the decision to live as a member of Jubilee Partners had everything to do with the Jesus he met at Koinonia, another community founded by Clarence Jordan, a farmer and New Testament scholar from Georgia who devoted his life to asking what Jesus' movement looked like in mid-twentieth-century Georgia. According to Jordan, Jesus would have been lynched for trying to integrate the church in Georgia. This Jesus taught his disciples to fast, Jordan wrote, because "fasting is the opposite of slowing"; it is a "speeding up toward the kingdom."

Just as an Olympic swimmer shaves his body hair to cut down on drag in the water, followers of Jesus strip themselves of excess baggage and forgo meals now and again for the sake of rushing ahead toward the new creation that God is giving us even now. Fasting, then, is not a denial of food's goodness, but rather a joining of ourselves with God's longing that there might be food enough for everyone in a world that has been redeemed.

Learning to Name Our Problem

It is Friday, and I am trying to keep our community's weekly fast — no food before dinner on the day when Jesus died. Hunger is visceral. If you're used to eating breakfast at seven, your stomach will remind you by eight that you've missed it. By ten it sends a message marked "urgent." By noon, it's howling. This feels wrong. Your body rises up against the injustice of what now appears to be an overly spiritual commitment made in a fit of irrational religious zeal. People cannot survive without food. What were you thinking?

But like anything you practice, fasting is more doable than it seems at first. You learn to pace yourself, to avoid caffeine, to not go for the sugar rush of fruit juice early in the day. You learn what the malnourished know too well: that hunger stops screaming after a while—that it can, to an extent, be managed. You go on.

Your energy isn't what you are used to, so you have to slow down. Earlier in the day, when you were trying to distract yourself from the gnawing in your gut, you rushed through to-do lists, eager to get things done. Your goal was clear and you were fasting toward it with clarity of purpose and singleness of heart.

Now, you are weak. Experience says, "You can do this. Don't give up." But this unalterable weakness—this basic vulnerability—is harder to endure than the hunger pangs you pushed through like an athlete. You have no push left. A runner at the point of exhaustion, you have come to the limit of your own strength. By way of fasting you come face-to-face with the truth that eating points to: you are a dependent creature, and you do well to remember it.

But you don't. When your belly is full, your body strong, your bank account in the black—when all is generally as we would like it to be in our lives, we forget our contingency. We despise our membership in creation and run from communion with our Creator. Though a desire as basic as hunger points us toward the life we were made for, we are too easily overcome by the longing to transcend our limits and become something more than we are.

This is why we fast: to confess what Christian teaching calls "original sin" and to proclaim our hope that we have been saved from it.

To help us name our problem, the Bible tells a story about eating. After God had created everything and said that it was good, God created humans and called us "very good." We were made for life with God in a garden where our feet touched the soil and our lives were directed by the same voice that first breathed life into our bodies. In this garden, God said, we could eat from any tree except the tree of "the knowledge of good and bad." What we knew from the mouth of God was that every created thing—every inch of the world we lived in—was good. The hunger that stirred within us pointed toward a good creation we were made to enjoy. Knowing only good, we could love God and do what we wanted.

But one day, as Genesis tells the story, a crafty serpent raised the question, "Did God really say, 'You must not eat from any tree in the garden?'" (Genesis 3:1). The wording of the question is tricky. Did God really say that we cannot eat from *any* tree—that we cannot eat at all? Of course not. The garden is our home; its food is ours to consume and enjoy. Why, then, is there *any* tree that we should not eat from? Why is the fruit of the tree of knowledge off limits? Why, that is, should there be *any* limit to our desires?

The serpent has an answer: "God knows that when you eat from it your eyes will be opened, and you will be like God, knowing good and evil" (3:5). Though we know that we are created in God's image, we are equally clear up to this point in the human story that there is a basic difference between us and God. While we have freedom to choose from the good gifts of the garden, to name the animals, to celebrate one another, we are not like God in that we do not have the capacity to judge independently. To the human creature in Eden, something is true or good or beautiful not because we judge it to be so over and against some standard, but only because God has said, "It is good."

God's word is our standard. Creation is good because God says so, and we need know nothing else.

This is the blessing of our original vocation. We were made to enjoy the earth and watch over it, to share life with God and keep God's commandments. We were made to know only good. We did not have to know the bad.

But the serpent interjects the thought that this vocation with its inherit limits may not be a gift—that our existence as creatures might somehow hold us back from our full potential as God's image bearers. The serpent tempts us to doubt God's word. Suddenly, the trust of communion is broken. Things begin to fall apart.

On this side of our rebellion (usually called "the Fall"), we can ask all kinds of questions that are tainted with the doubt that the serpent introduced: Why did God create a serpent with questions like this? Why did God allow the first humans to be tempted? If the tree of knowledge was to be our downfall, why did God plant it in the garden?

The traditional answer to questions like this is that God preferred a world where creatures might choose to love God freely to a world where there was no possibility of exceeding our limits. God offers us life as a gift, not a sentence. While this may be true, and even helpful in our understanding of human freedom, it is also worth noting that questions like these are only possible because of the broken trust that results from us eating the fruit God told us not to eat.

We call this sin "original" because it was committed by the

very first humans—the great-grandparents to whom all of us can trace our family trees. "Sin entered the world through one man," the apostle Paul says (see Romans 5:12). Our tendency to doubt God's word and trust our own judgment is thus present in the first generation of humanity. But this means sin is also original in another sense—and one we naturally take much more personally. We are, each of us, also sinners from the start. Though the nature of freedom is such that I constantly choose to sin, and am therefore responsible for it, it is also the case that there was no time in my life when I did not know the vast system of broken trust and fragmented relationships that the story of the Fall describes.

However well I might have been loved by my parents, I am the product of countless broken relationships.

My own desires—even one as basic as hunger—are twisted by this condition. Just as the first humans had no standard apart from God's word by which they could rightly judge good from bad, I have no anvil upon which I can straighten the twisted desires of my will. In short, my want-er is broken. Nothing makes this as clear to me as the practice of fasting.

My hunger pangs have subsided, and the afternoon stretches before me. I no longer have to think about my fast. I can get on with my work. But, I think to myself, I could probably get more done if I had more energy. I think about how important the work that I'm doing is. Fasting has its value, yes, but haven't I already done the real work of fasting? Wouldn't it be more efficient for me to have a little snack and keep going? I know my limits; isn't that the most important thing? I can go on with questions like this for hours. I am a son of Adam, well practiced in the arts of self-deception.

Fasting is a struggle to the very end. To do it is to join your most basic desires with the ancient prayer: "Lord Jesus Christ, Son of God, have mercy on me, a sinner."

Turning toward Hope

From its earliest days, God's movement has been a repentance movement—a "calling out" so that we might learn a different way of life. God calls Noah and his family to turn from their normal lives and enter into the ark, not only so that they can be saved from the flood waters but also so that they can learn what faithful existence with God and other creatures looks like. What Noah learns in a forty-day crash course is expanded to a forty-year wilderness school when God calls Israel out of Egypt. It is not enough to be set free from bondage to this world's broken systems, God says. It is not enough to simply get out of Egypt. We have to get Egypt out of us. This requires a turning—a process of repentance that leads to new life. It is a turning toward hope.

The twentieth-century theologian Karl Barth said that we can only know sin "on our way out." To confess our sin is a sign that our bondage to this world's broken systems has been interrupted. Greed is no longer normal. Violence is not simply reality. As common as these habits may be in my life and in our world, they do not have the last word. To call them sin is to see that they are a corruption of what we were made to be. They are the characteristics of a broken norm, a twisted reality. And this insight carries with it a revolutionary hope: *If the way things are is not the way things should be, then another world is possible.*

A world in which sin can be named is a world that is being redeemed.

Repentance movements carve out space for radical imagination. A place like Jubilee Partners isn't a commune for dropouts who've become dissatisfied with the rat race of climbing the ladder. It is, instead, a space where fasting from the conventional comforts of American life has clarified vision and sparked imagination for thousands of people. It is no accident that in the 1980s, when American foreign policy in Latin America was creating refugees who were denied political asylum in the United States, Jubilee Partners dreamed up a network of churches and communities across the U.S. and Canada who would offer hospitality to these homeless victims, pledging allegiance to a higher law of love. Such welcome was not only illegal in the eyes of most Americans; it was unimaginable. But years of fasting toward the kingdom and learning to name our collective sin made it possible for the folks at Jubilee to invite others to join them in a Sanctuary Movement toward a better hope.

In his *Rule* for life together in Christian community, St. Benedict of Nursia wrote that one of the tools for the Lord's service at every monk's disposal is "to love fasting."[6] Though not the easiest tool in the box, this love of fasting is for Benedict an aid in pursuit of the monastic way of life—a life of constant turning, a way of repentance. For all the dour images we have of repentance (think of medieval monks whipping themselves or puritanical church ladies shaking their fingers), the overwhelming witness of Benedictine communities has been one of hospitality, service, and love. Trace our modern hospitals, hospices, universities, and social service programs to their historic roots, and you will often find a community of men or women who were committed to living Benedict's *Rule*. They loved fasting not for its own sake, but for the hope of a better world.

When Jesus returns from his forty-day fast in the wilderness, repentance is on his mind. "For the kingdom of God is at hand," Mark's gospel records as his inaugural message, "repent" (1:15 KJV). Jesus has gone head-to-head with the twisted ways of a broken world, refusing the temptations of economic power, political position, and miraculous authority. In each case, his only reply to the temptation of the evil one is a word from the Lord. Jesus defeats the devil in the same way he created the world—by the power of God's word.

For the reader who knows the story of God's people, the gospel writers are echoing the fast of Moses in their presentation of Jesus' forty-day fast. Moses, too, fasted for forty days in the wilderness at Horeb, before receiving the Ten Commandments and bringing them down from the mountain as an enduring sign of God's presence among the people of Israel. This gift of the law was, once again, a word from God—direct communication so that we might know what is good and "keep it" as we follow the way that leads to life. But this word is given in the context of rebellion, even as God's people are worshiping a golden calf at the base of the mountain where Moses has gone to meet with God. So much for restoring Eden.

Though we are sustained by the food we eat, God's people fast as a reminder that we do not live by bread alone, but by every word of the Lord. Created by God's command and animated by divine breath, we cannot live apart from God's word. But twisted by sin and a history of rebellion, we do not receive God's word as a gift. "No one will be declared righteous in God's sight by the works of the law," Paul says in his letter to the Romans; "rather, through the law we become conscious of our sin" (3:20). A way of repentance doesn't offer a program by which we learn to fix ourselves. Instead, it helps us to be honest about who we are and what we need in a world hell-bent on rebellion against our Creator.

One of the most enduring critiques of Christianity is that a faith that promises so much delivers so little. Ask the average unchurched person why they don't participate in a faith community, and they do not typically say it's because they don't believe in God. Most people aren't even put off by Jesus. It's Christians that really bother them. "They act like they're part of some 'holy huddle,' but most of them are just as selfish and mean as the rest of us. When they get all fired up with their righteous indignation, Christians can be the meanest bunch of all." Gandhi said he liked the Christ he read about in the gospels; he just didn't like Christians.

When we fast, we remember that we are not perfect. We are not, as a matter of fact, even above average. We are, in truth, sinners in need of grace. Our only hope is a gracious God.

The church's first monastic movement, which arose out of the wilderness of the Egyptian desert, was marked by the practice of fasting. Accounts of all-night vigils, years of eating only one meal a day, and long stretches of silent prayer abound in the records we have from pilgrims who visited the desert mothers and fathers. By any measure, their way of life was austere. To most any modern person, it seems extreme. If the tendency of religion is to make people self-righteous, it would seem that these super-religious ascetics would be extremely so. But the witness of everyone who visited them for counsel was the opposite. They were some of the most gracious souls the world has ever known.

The story is told of an Abba Moses, who, after living as a pirate in the desert and raiding caravans on lonesome roads, was converted by the witness of a community of monks. He joined their way of repentance and, hard as it was at first, gave himself to the ascetic practices of this peculiarly graceful community. Years later, when a brother was accused of misconduct in the community, Moses was invited to a meeting to discuss an appropriate penance for his wayward brother. He did not come. When called again, he came reluctantly, carrying a leaky jug of water. "Why did you bring this leaky jug?" the brothers asked Moses. His reply: "My sins trail out behind me wherever I go. Who am I to judge my brother?"[7]

The nonjudgmentalism of the desert tradition is a mark of those who fast well. It reminds us that a way of repentance, however seriously we take it, leads away from the self-righteousness of holy huddles toward the hope of a future interrupted by grace. Dorothy Day, a founder of the Catholic Worker movement, was fond of saying, "Don't call me a saint. I don't want to be dismissed so easily." The voluntary poverty she embraced to welcome strangers and visit those in prison was not a pious perch from which to judge others. It was an extreme response to an even more extreme grace.

We do not fast because we're saints, but because we're sinners. We know our world is broken and we are all wrapped up in its brokenness. Like addicts in recovery, we confess that recovery must begin with us. Laid bare before a God who loves us, we come to know the transformative power of gracious love. And we know that our recovery cannot be complete until we join God's movement to repair the society that made us sick. "All shall be well, and all manner of things shall be well," said Julian of Norwich, a medieval anchorite who practiced an extreme asceticism. We fast toward this hope, however slow our turning may feel.

Suffering with Christ

At the edge of a pasture on their farm, the Jubilee Partners have a small cemetery. A founding member is buried there, alongside refugees who have died on the farm. With them in the ground, there are also men who have been executed by the state of Georgia. Jubilee Partners have named an end to state-sponsored killing as part of the new world they are fasting toward. They have befriended men on death row, advocated for them in their appeals process, and prayed with them as they've struggled with both their histories and their fate. Long before national civil rights leaders and celebrities got behind the "I AM TROY DAVIS" campaign in 2011, Jubilee Partners were visiting Troy and others on death row. The community has learned something about a way of repentance that leads to hope from these brothers. But this cemetery remains as a reminder of death's power. Here lie men who killed, condemned to death by a system that has no hope for them.

To fast is not only to focus; it is also to suffer. Yes, we strip off extra weight to rush toward the kingdom. Yes, we clarify our understanding of who we are and what we're called to be. Yes, we turn from our desperate attempts to feed ourselves to the hope of bread that satisfies. But we also suffer. We feel the pain of hunger and experience the loss of food or rest or comfort we expect, even need. Like the Jubilee Partners, we join ourselves with the sufferings of others. When we fast, their pain is ours. We feel it in our bones.

After upbraiding Israel for keeping fasts that were little more than religious performance, God speaks through the prophet Isaiah about the true purpose of fasting. "Is not this the kind of fast I have chosen," the Lord declares: "to loose the chains of injustice and untie the chords of the yoke, to set the oppressed free and break every yoke? Is it not to share your food with the hungry and to provide the poor wanderer with shelter—when you see the naked, to clothe him, and not to turn away from your own flesh and blood?" (58:6–7).

If fasting serves to clarify our vision, it is so we might see this one thing and see it clearly: when fellow creatures suffer, we suffer. The actions fasting compels us toward are both works of justice and works of mercy—helping the victims of broken systems and getting in the way of those systems' violence. But this work is never done, and a commitment to "not turn away from our own flesh and blood" means that we will bury friends whose lives are snuffed out by a culture of death. In the end, we will be buried with them. Our hope rests neither in avoiding suffering nor in accepting it, but in enduring it for the sake of a reward that we must pass through this present darkness to receive.

This peculiar approach to suffering is one that we learn from Jesus, though it is deeply rooted in the prophet Isaiah. The servant whom Isaiah anticipates as the hope of God's people is "a man of sorrows, and familiar with suffering" (53:3). He does not overcome evil by mounting a crusade against it. This servant does not beat our stubborn selfishness out of us. He understands the nature of our problem — that "each of us has turned to his own way" (53:6). What hope, then, does he offer? "The Lord has laid on him," Isaiah says, "the iniquity of us all" (53:6).

This is the root of what Christian teaching calls substitutionary atonement. Out of context, it is often derided as a cultic notion that betrays a cruel God. What kind of God, critics ask, would demand a substitute victim on which to exercise his wrath so that the rest of humanity does not have to suffer? What's more, what sort of twisted Father would ask this of his Son? Most people are not relieved to learn that Jesus had to suffer and die a cruel death so God would not damn them to hell.

But this is not the good news that Isaiah anticipated or that the New Testament proclaims. In the context of original sin, which Genesis has helped us to name, Isaiah's suffering servant is one who sees clearly the root of human violence. Though we are inextricably connected to others in the membership of creation, our relationships are fragmented by sin. The twisted desires which Adam and Eve pass on to their sons lead to murder in the second generation of humanity. And this conflict of personalities is quickly magnified to conflicts between societies after the confusion of languages at the Tower of Babel.

In short, we are all caught up in a cycle of violence. Each selfish act inevitably affects our fellow human beings and, in something of a domino effect, leads them to react in some selfish (and self-defensive) way. Isaiah sees with prophetic clarity that the only hope of ending this cycle would be for someone to take sin upon them self without passing it on to others. But who could muster the inner resources to suffer without retaliation—to endure the world's violence in love?

The answer the New Testament proposes is God. Given the selfishness in our DNA, there was no hope that any of us—not even Mother Teresa or Gandhi or the Dali Lama —was ever going to be able to interrupt the cycle of violence by only returning good for evil. Thus the substitution that animates the hope of Christianity is the incarnation—the belief that God took on human flesh in Jesus Christ to do for us what we could not collectively or individually do for ourselves. "Being in very nature God," Paul explains, Jesus "did not consider equality with God something to be used to his own advantage; rather, he made himself nothing by taking the very nature of a servant" (Philippians 2:6–7). This is a servant that attentive readers of Isaiah recognize.

God acts definitely in Jesus to become our suffering servant, to overcome evil with good. He lives the life of the true human being, attentive to every word of God and faithful to every relationship with other people and the world around him. To people who have been crushed by this world's broken systems, Jesus' life is a welcome interruption—an eruption, even, of good news. But to the powers who are invested in the way the broken system works, Jesus is an enemy who must be killed.

Jesus' willingness to suffer a criminal's death on the cross, having done absolutely nothing wrong, is the ultimate sign of God's love for us. This is the substitution that both atones for our sins and makes it possible for us to live at one with even our enemies. Thus, *substitutionary atonement* is not an embarrassing dogma, but genuine good news.

We live in a world where the cycle of death has been interrupted by true life. The lie of retributive violence has been revealed, its power defeated. But the cycle continues. As clear as the New Testament is about Christ's victory over the power of death, it also names our world's continued submission to that same power. "The last enemy to be destroyed," Paul says, "is death" (1 Corinthians 15:26). We live presently in the time between Christ's victory and death's ultimate defeat. We fast toward a new creation where justice rolls down like waters and righteousness like an ever-flowing stream.

Because we are not there yet, we suffer.

Because our lives have been caught up in the life of Jesus, we rejoice to suffer with him.

Writing to a fellowship of the early church, Paul says, "I rejoice in what I am suffering for you, and I fill up in my flesh what is still lacking in regard to Christ's afflictions, for the sake of his body, which is the church" (Colossians 1:24). This approach to affliction is unique both in its tone and its perspective. Though suffering is common to us all, it is surprising —disconcerting, even—to hear someone *rejoice* in suffering. Our bodies cry out that suffering is wrong, concurring with a basic sense of justice. Though we may not always escape its sting, mind and body agree that suffering is not right. How, then, could anyone find joy in suffering? Again, the question: why would anyone willingly give up comfort and influence to live with refugees for $15 a week—to be buried, in the end, with victims of execution?

The peculiar tone of joy in Paul's declaration is tied to the perspective that is gained by seeing that we are invited to suffer with Christ as members of his living body. To "fill up in my flesh what is still lacking in regard to Christ's affliction" is to see that I too can return good for evil, not because I have overcome the selfishness of original sin, but because I have been loved by One who takes my sin, offering only forgiveness in return.

To be loved by Jesus is to be joined with his body—in the imagery of the ancient church, it is to be buried in the waters of baptism and raised to new life in the living body of Christ. Here the domino effect is reversed. The wrongs that used to inspire acts of revenge or passive-aggression are now absorbed by a loving God through those who are made Christ's body in the world. No, the aftershocks of the Fall have not yet ceased. We have not yet finished feeling the ripple effects of original sin. But we know that sin is defeated because we know the One who has suffered without retaliation. In him, we rejoice to fill up in our own flesh the affliction that is yet to be absorbed by God's infinite love.

To love fasting is not to enjoy pain, but to see that it has a purpose. When we embrace the suffering of our world with Christ, we can celebrate with joy that the worst of our brokenness has been (and is being) redeemed. "The extreme greatness of Christianity," wrote twentieth-century mystic Simone Weil, "lies in the fact that it does not seek a supernatural remedy for suffering, but a supernatural use for it."

We fast to join our bodies with the hunger of the malnourished child in Lima's barrio, with the Congolese mother's cry for peace. We go down to the dirt with those who are condemned to death because we know that in Christ we will be raised with them to a life that cannot end. Even when it hurts, we fast to hold onto this hope.

CHAPTER 4

Why We Make Promises

IN A SPARSE LIVING ROOM, JUST OFF A BUSY STREET, A YOUNG
man kneels on hard wood floor, his head bowed, oil dripping
from his hair. Standing around him with their hands on his
head, his back, his shoulders, a small group is praying. They
are asking God to bless the promise this young man has made
—"to persevere with these people in this place." Minutes ago,
one of them read from Psalm 133:

> How good and pleasant it is
>   when God's people live together in unity!
> It is like precious oil poured on the head,
>   running down on the beard,
> running down on Aaron's beard,
>   down on the collar of his robe. (1–3)

This oil is anointing oil, like the oil that marked Aaron as
a priest—like the perfume that Mary of Bethany poured on
Jesus' feet, signifying him as one who was set apart for God's
service. This is precious oil, dripping down on holy ground.
It is precious not so much for its market value as for the commitment it marks.

"Do you promise to submit to the Holy Spirit as discerned in this community?" a leader asked the young man as he presented himself for membership. His "I do" was echoed by the community, who pledged their commitment to him. Now they are touching, united in prayer, the oil of these promises on each of their hands. This is a solemn vow before their God.

If a passerby in this low-income, inner-city neighborhood were to peek in the window and witness this scene, she would probably be suspicious. Who besides gangs and cults perform ritual acts of initiation, asking members to commit their whole life to something? If she knew this young man, she would likely be concerned. Has he been brainwashed by this group? We are leery of organizations that ask too much of people. We worry about friends who submit to extreme demands. Vows can be dangerous.

Yet, for most of the history of the church, small groups of monks and nuns have welcomed members in ceremonies like this, making lifelong promises in the service of God and the church. In his *Rule*, St. Benedict of Nursia instructs communities to test those who come seeking membership, leaving them to knock at the door for four or five days. Only if these seekers are persistent should they be invited into the community for a short time, after which the *Rule* is to be thoroughly explained to them. Then, if they want, they can practice living this way of life. Through various stages, this testing continues. But when someone is finally ready to join, the commitment is total: she declares her intent to the group, bows at their feet in prayer, and leaves everything, even the clothes on her back, for the new life she has chosen in community.

Extreme as this may seem to the modern observer, monastic vows sound somewhat familiar to anyone who has been to a wedding ceremony or themselves said "I do" before God and community. In both its commitments of marriage and celibacy, the church calls its members to make promises about who we will be faithful to in our daily living. Our lives are not our own. We have been made living members of the body of Christ. Nothing could be more extreme, yet our new life gets fleshed out in terms of particular relationships and the promises that make them possible. To learn to live "in Christ" is to learn to make promises and keep them.

But we live in a world marked by infidelity, each of us debilitated in our incapacity to do what we say we will do. While we may suspect others of simply lying when they do not keep their promises, we each know from our own experience that we often fail to do things that we fully intended to do when we said we would do them. Indeed, we may have never consciously chosen *not* to do them. We just forgot. Or got distracted by other things. Yet, in our relationships with other people these broken promises add up, creating walls of mistrust on the already fragmented landscape of our shared existence. We learn to confess both the evil we've done and "the things we have left undone" because we know our will is weak from the start.

Infidelity is a tendency deep within us. But it also comes to us through the constant barrage of powers at work in this world's broken systems. Because sex sells we are inundated daily by the suggestive poses of women and men to whom we're not only not committed but whom we do not even know. Their images come to our senses not as icons in which we might glimpse the divine but as products to be consumed. This pornographic imagination is extended to real estate, destinations, entertainment events, and even educational opportunities. Our broken economy does not invite us to ask how we might be faithful to our people and place but rather how we might use them to satisfy our base desires. Infidelity is sold to us as a good.

In his classic text *On Christian Doctrine*, St. Augustine of Hippo made an important distinction in Christian thinking between something that is to be enjoyed for its own sake and something that is to be used for the sake of enjoying something else. Unlike the modern philosopher Immanuel Kant, who argued that human beings are ends in themselves, Augustine claimed that all creatures—even fellow humans—are to be "used" for the sake of enjoying God. Everything God has made is good, and people are *very* good, according to the creation story. But every good thing is meant to point us toward the greatest Good, the Giver of all good things. The earth, then, is charged with the glory of God, heaven shouting out to us at every turn.

But we defile the holy when we love good things for our own sake, deadening our sense of intimacy and connection with God. When we use people and places to serve ourselves, we are not only untrue to our fellow creatures. We also distance ourselves from the Creator and from the part of ourselves that cries out for connection with the divine. Infidelity unravels the intricate fabric of the universe.

To make promises is to proclaim that a culture of mistrust has been interrupted by One whom we can trust. It is to live as a sign of God's faithfulness, even as we struggle to grow into fidelity ourselves. We make promises because we've glimpsed a picture of hope and know that it points us toward the life we were made for.

Marked by Covenant

The ring I wear on the fourth finger of my left hand is a public sign of the promises my wife, Leah, and I made in marriage. When I turn it with my thumb, as I often do by habit, I think of Leah, our kids, and the commitments that make our shared life possible. I've worn this ring for a decade now. Its significance is deeply personal. But at the same time, I wear this ring for all to see on a hand I use to carry groceries, play basketball, and pass the offering plate at church. Though my ring is personally significant, it also serves as a public announcement of the promises I've made to God, my wife, our family, and community. This ring marks me as a married man.

In traditional monasticism, there have likewise been signs to mark the commitments of those who make vows. As early as the Egyptian desert, the habit was worn by monks as a sign charged with meaning. In his *Praktikos*, the desert father Evagrius Ponticus explains how the cowl (or hood) symbolizes God's charity; the cross-shaped scapular, faith; the monk's belt marks rejection of impurity; and his staff is to lean on as he leans on the Lord. "We see then," Evagrius concludes, "that the monk's habit is a kind of compendious symbol of all that we have described." In a sense, it sums up his life. As the mark of monastic vocation, a habit points beyond itself to a way of life that finds its end in God. To read it as a sign is to direct ourselves toward contemplation.

We make promises because they mark us as people who are turning from the rebellion of original sin to life with God in the membership of a new creation. To say "I do" in a world marked by infidelity is to stand out as a living sign that faithfulness is possible. It is possible because we know a God who makes promises and keeps them. We know this because we know the story of this God's relationship with the people called Israel.

The story of creation and fall that we have already explored is a cosmic story that aims to explain everything. It presents us with an infinite categorical distinction between Creator and creation and addresses the classic problem of evil by naming all that's wrong in the world as a corruption of God's good creation. By itself, this story might be told as a universal history of the world. But as we have it, this account of origins is the peculiar memory of a particular people. It is the foundation for their strange sojourn with God, and thus for our understanding of this God's way in the world. We cannot understand the peculiar nature of Christian hope, then, without knowing the story of the God who makes covenant with Israel.

The first covenant that this Creator God makes is not with Israel, but with the whole earth. After establishing Noah's ark as a school for living, God looks down on a world still drying from the great flood and makes a promise: "Never again." As a sign of this covenant with every living creature, God puts a rainbow in the heavens—the full spectrum of light to encircle the earth after a hard rain. It is, as one rabbi notes, a bow pointed away from the earth. It is a sign to follow the rain, a visible reminder of God's promise that the chaos of waters will not overwhelm the whole earth again.

This promise points us forward. We follow the arch of the rainbow, even if not to a pot of gold, because its promise bends toward hope. If the Creator will not destroy the earth again, then this God must have a plan to redeem it. But how? The first covenant points toward the second.

But the second is not a covenant with all creation. It is, instead, a promise to one man, Abram. In the language of his people, Abram's name means "great father." But God calls him Abraham—"the father of many"—promising, "I will bless you ... and all people on earth will be blessed through you" (Genesis 12:2, 3). The irony of Abram's name when we meet him is that this great father does not, in fact, have any children. A herder who was apparently skilled in the tribal warfare of his time, Abram showed some promise (at least in the memory of his descendents). But he lacked the one thing that every man in the ancient world needed if he was to be considered great. He had no son.

Still, God promises that Abram will become the father of many—that a great nation will emerge from his lineage and that this people will bless the whole world. The hope that the first covenant points toward is alive in the second. Here, though, it takes on a peculiar shape: God promises to work through a particular people who will learn to live by trust in God, not by their own ability to judge the good from the bad. "Abram believed the LORD," Genesis says, "and he credited it to him as righteousness" (15:6).

But Abraham is like the father who comes to Jesus asking for his son to be healed. "Everything is possible for one who believes," Jesus says to the father. His reply: "I do believe; help me overcome my unbelief" (Mark 9:23, 24). The challenge of faith isn't so much to trust God's promises when we hear them as it is to continue trusting them when it does not appear to our best judgment that they are being fulfilled. Belief is not, in the end, an abstract consideration of whether I think God exists or whether the evidence suggests that Jesus did in fact get up from the grave. It is, instead, a man sitting with his wife, desperate to have a child, listening to the doctor say it is impossible. Faith is that man saying, "God can make a way," and continuing to live as if he will become the father of many.

"I do believe; help me overcome my unbelief." It could have just as well been Abraham's prayer. For though he trusts God's promise, he cannot avoid the doubts that come with the passing years. Our father in the faith shows us from the start how difficult trust is, how easy it can be to trust another way, even if only for a moment. Sarah comes to Abraham with an idea: maybe God wants to give them a son through her servant, Hagar. It was, no doubt, Sarah's own feeling of insufficiency that first whispered the idea to her, like the serpent in Eden. "Surely God didn't mean *you* would have a son." The thought, once planted as a seed of doubt, grows like a weed into a scheme of mistrust. A child is born, and with him enmity enters Abraham and Sarah's house. Again, as in Eden, things fall apart.

The great temptation of religion is always self-righteousness. People who are into God like to turn our notions about God into beliefs we can use to justify ourselves over and against someone else. That is, we like to be right. And we confuse right with righteous. But if we pay attention to the Bible's story about Abraham's faith, it's clear that the people God chooses are not picked for their exceptional ability to get things right.

Yes, God's people believe. But not without their unbelief. Immediately after God's promise in the rainbow, Noah gets drunk and embarrasses his sons. After Abraham has left everything, betting his life on God's promise, he sleeps with the servant girl, trying for a son by any means necessary. God doesn't make covenant with us because we get things right. God makes promises because God is good.

The difficult thing for all of us who know the good and the bad is to simply trust that God is good. To survive this broken, twisted world, we have learned to make a thousand judgments about whom we can trust, how we negotiate the power we have, when we should fight and when we need to run. I'm sympathetic with Abraham and the father who brings his son to Jesus. As a father myself, I make judgments every day in the hope that my children can flourish. I want to protect their little spirits, their precious smiles. But it's a hard, cold world out there. I've known the bad, and I'd love to save them from it.

The mark of God's covenant with Abraham is a peculiar one. Though it is for the blessing of all creation, it is not in the heavens for all to see. It is, instead, in Abraham's flesh. "Every male among you shall be circumcised," God says. This is the sign to mark the promise that Sarah and Abraham, who have no children, will be the parents of many. It is a wound in the procreative flesh of every man in their household—a wound that not only endangers them against attack (how can they defend themselves if every man is recovering from such a procedure?) but also makes sex unimaginable. When time seems to be running out, God gives Abraham a wound to remind him that his promised son will come not from his own strength, but from the power of God's promise.

The instructions of this covenant are clear: as intimate and personal as this sign is for Abraham, it is to be re-inscribed in every son of Abraham's line on the eighth day after their birth. In Jewish tradition, it is said that a baby boy does not become fully human until he is circumcised on the eighth day. From birth, we are marked by original sin. But on the eighth day—on the day that follows God's Sabbath, the day of new creation—children of the promise are marked with a wound that points toward our trust in the power of God.

The sign of this covenant points to radical dependence.

We have hope that our world is being redeemed, even when our own faith falters, because God is able to make a way out of no way. We make promises not because we are masters of fidelity but because our lives have been caught up in the life of a God whose promises cannot fail.

To Be a People

In the time before Jesus, after Alexander the Great had conquered Palestine for the Greeks, *gymnasiums* were established in the land that God had promised to Abraham and his children. As centers of education, these institutions of the occupying power were meant to train men in the Greek way of life. They were not only cultural centers that promoted the ideals of Greece, they were training centers where bodies were exercised to embody those ideals. Like the fitness centers of our modern cities, these gyms put perfect bodies on display, giving everyone an image of what they should strive to be.

In the Greek gym, men exercised nude. So the mark of the covenant was put on public display, exposing children of Abraham and setting them apart in a way that could only bring shame. Circumcision was foolishness to the Greeks. In the gymnasium, there was no way for sons of Abraham to hide the fact that they were a people set apart.

As children of covenant, God's people make promises because our lives have been claimed by a God who is faithful. Our vows are rooted in a particular understanding of who God is and what it means to trust God's word. But to trust our lives to this God is to stand out among other people in this world. Though we share a common history with other humans in Adam and Noah, we look different to people who have not been interrupted by Abraham's story. To be marked by covenant is not only to carry a wound that points us toward our dependence on God but also to share life together as a people set apart. We make promises to learn what faith means, for sure. But that is not all. We also make promises so we can know what it means to be God's peculiar people in the world.

Long before their land was occupied by the Greeks, Abraham's children learned to be God's people in the wilderness. Forced by famine to leave their land, they spent four hundred years in Egypt, remembering God's promises but not sure how they would be fulfilled in the strange land where Pharaoh ruled. When God's people grew in number and the people of Egypt were threatened by their size, Pharaoh made a decree that all the male children of Abraham (Hebrews, he called them) should be killed. Rather than mark them as children of promise, Egyptian midwives marked Hebrew babies for death.

One mother who could not bear the thought put her son in a waterproofed basket and sent him sailing down the Nile. Maybe some Egyptian mother would have mercy and raise him as her own. As it happened, Pharaoh's own daughter heard the crying basket when she was taking her river bath, and the baby became grandson to Pharaoh by adoption. He was called Moses, which means "drawn out." None of this was by accident. Years later, after meeting Abraham's God at a burning bush in the desert, Moses would return to Pharaoh's household and draw the Hebrew children out of Egypt, leading them back to the land promised to Abraham. There, they would be a people.

But before God's people could make a life together in the Promised Land, they had to listen again to God's promises. "I am making a covenant with you," God says to Moses, instructing him to write down words of instruction for the community to govern itself (Exodus 34:10). "Pay attention," the story seems to say. This is a word from God.

Moses receives two tablets with ten commandments — ten good words from God. This is the founding document of Israel's law. While Moses will write many more words, these tablets of stone, brought down from the mountain, will be the sign of this covenant between God and Israel. The entire legal code of this people will be determined not by the collective wisdom of case law or the declaration of founding fathers, but by the Word that spoke creation into existence.

Israel is to be a people marked by trust in the command of God.

Like circumcision, the law sets God's people apart among the nations. They are to welcome the alien stranger in their midst, not because this is best for national security but because they are called to remember that their father Abraham was a wandering Aramean. They are to keep Sabbath every seventh day and seventh year, culminating in a year of Jubilee every fiftieth year, not because this will build a strong economy but because it reflects the justice and mercy of their God. They must abstain from pork and a great number of other foods not because those foods aren't healthy, but because they are unholy. God says not to eat them, so they don't.

Living under the law, Israel learns how to translate faith into a life together. Abraham believed God, yes, but what does it look like for a people to live as God commands—to walk in the way that leads to life? The Mosaic covenant is God's first promise with condition: "If you pay attention to these laws and are careful to follow them, then the LORD your God will keep his covenant of love with you" (Deuteronomy 7:12). God's promise finds concrete form in this particular way of life. "Do *this*," God says, "and you will live."

The tradition of vows in monastic community has always been tied to a Rule of Life. Monks and nuns do not promise poverty, chastity, and obedience in the abstract as ideals that they would like to live out in whatever circumstances they happen to find themselves. Monastic vows are always promises made to God and a community under a particular Rule. These promises have concrete meaning within a way of life that is shared by a people. Poverty doesn't mean holding money loosely or owning things without letting them own you. It means giving the money and possessions you have inherited and earned away, joining a group of others who have done the same, and trusting God to provide for you in that particular community for the rest of your life.

In the same way, the promises that Christians make in marriage only make sense within the way of life we learn by being part of a people called church. We know what it means to give our body to another only to the extent that we have learned what it means for a community to claim our bodies in baptism. This will be a journey filled with joy as husband and wife delight in one another's bodies and welcome children as a fruit of that delight.

But Christian marriage is about more than what feels natural and good. Because we have died with Christ, we know that giving our body to another will mean bearing with them through afflictions—"in sickness and in health," as the traditional vows have it. Because we are members of God's family by adoption, we know we may have children who do not look like us. Because we follow a Lord who was executed, we know that we won't be able to make everything work out alright for our families in this world.

We know these things, as the monastic witness reminds us, because we are the spiritual descendents of the people called Israel. Both God's promises and ours in return find their content in the particularities of a shared way of life. We cannot find our way with God alone. While intimacy with God is always deeply personal, it cannot be private. "Me and Jesus" will not work. We're in this together, or we're not in it at all.

If the Mosaic covenant is not enough to interrupt us on this point, it may be that Islam will. Since September 11, 2001, we in the West have become painfully aware of the fact that Islamic extremists do not make a distinction between personal convictions and political imagination. But if we listen to the millions of Muslims who are not extremists but fellow children of Abraham with whom we have much in common, we will learn that they are equally confused by the separation of faith and politics in the West. "My personal religion," makes no sense to them. They know it is a contradiction of faith to say, "Let's live together and keep our faith to ourselves."

We can learn from our Muslim neighbors what Israel learned at Sinai: to trust God is to join a community of people who make promises. Our promises find their meaning in the patterns and habits of the way of life we share together. Because this Way has been revealed to us, it is as much a gift as the promise that first inspired our faith. But because it is what makes us a people, this Way is not optional. To trust our God is to pay attention and keep the commandments that make us a people set apart in this world.

For the Life of the World

A post-college group from a local church is gathered in the living room, just off that busy street, sitting on the hardwood floor where a young man knelt to promise his life to this community. This group is trying to make sense of his commitment, and those of others like him. Why would anyone promise their life to God in community? They are from a dozen states and two other countries — young professionals and graduate students, all of them shaped by a low-commitment culture that nevertheless has lofty ideals. They graduated from schools that told them either they were to go out, work hard, and run the world or they were to go out and work even harder to change it. They are ambitious young people who have, somehow, been fascinated by Jesus. One of them, an accountant, tries to name the tension.

"So, you've committed to stay here. How long are we talking?"

"We're here for life," one community member says.

She tries to clarify: "Is this like a five-year commitment? Ten years?"

"We don't know how long we'll live, but we plan to die here."

For the young accountant, this doesn't compute. She has worked hard to calculate possibilities, to manage futures, to keep her options open in pursuit of the best possible outcome. Ours is a broken world of sharp edges and hard breaks, she knows. She has read of the millions who are dying from poverty, of the wars that are raging in a dozen countries, of the exploitation in human trafficking, of our global environmental crisis. "For God so loved the world," she remembers reading also, and she knows she cannot sit idly in the comfort of her middle-class existence. Surely God wants her to do something. But in a world of so many possibilities, how could anyone commit to one place—and for their whole life long?

Saturated as our story is in covenant, the truth is that all of us—even committed, church-going Christians—are steeped in a culture of contracts that is deeply suspicious of promises. As we've already noted, we are bad at doing what we say we will do, and we know this, each of us. The collective legal codes of cultures all around the world attest to the fact that this tendency to infidelity is not a recent shortcoming in human history. Yet, with the increasing individualism that has emerged from a modern notion of rights and freedom, community safeguards against selfishness and abuse have deteriorated, leaving us with the sole defense of our current legal system—the contract.

To its credit, the contract is excellent at clarifying the terms of commitments. Each party to a contract knows what they are expected to do and what they can expect from others. It is written out in black and white. And because we know that people do not always do what we say we will do, our contracts also spell out terms for what will happen if any party fails to keep their promise. Ultimately, every contract has a dissolution policy that outlines from the very start what the relationship will look like if it ultimately falls apart. Every contract, then, is conditional.

God's story of covenant is an interruption to this logic. God's promise to Noah and to Abraham—to all creation and to all the children of faith—is not conditional. It is a promise that reveals something about who our God is—"gracious and compassionate, slow to anger and abounding in love, and he relents from sending calamity" (Joel 2:13). Though the Mosaic covenant, which fleshes out life with God under a law, does depend on God's people following the good Way that is given to us, the hope of the story is not that we will buckle down and achieve faithfulness, but that a Messiah will come who can establish God's reign and that, as the Lord says through the prophet Jeremiah, "I will put my law in their minds and write it on their hearts" (31:33). We will make promises and keep them because our God is great enough to make faithfulness possible, even among broken people like us.

For the apostle Paul, the Christian life is possible only because it is a life "in Christ." Jesus matters to those who know the story of covenant because Jesus bridges the divide between Creator and creation, fulfilling in his two natures both sides of the covenant that makes us who we are.

As God, Jesus keeps his promise not to destroy all creation, but to save it through the particular people of Abraham.

As a Jewish man, Jesus is circumcised on the eighth day and keeps the law that was given at Sinai, showing that it is truly written on his heart for the sake of the whole world.

"In him," Paul writes to the church, "you were also circumcised, in the putting off of the sinful nature, not with a circumcision performed by human hands. Your whole self ruled by the flesh was put off when you were circumcised by Christ" (Colossians 2:11). The sign of the covenant is, as with Abraham, written on our flesh. But, echoing Jeremiah (4:4), Paul insists that it is a "circumcision of the heart" (Romans 2:29), marking us at the core of our being and redirecting our very desires toward new life.

Do those of us who have been baptized into Christ's body always keep the promises we make? No, we have not been made perfect. In their struggle to "be perfect ... as your heavenly Father is perfect" (Matthew 5:48), the mothers and fathers of the desert tradition came face-to-face with their weakness and infidelity. In that place of humility, they learned the grace that is given to us in Christ. "It is the property of angels not to fall," Abba Macedonius said. "It is the property of men to fall, and to rise again as often as this may happen." We make promises not because we will always be able to keep them, but because we trust a God who is faithful enough to always help us get up again.

This falling down and getting up, as undramatic as it may seem, is what the story of covenant teaches us to see as the most important thing any of us can ever do. If the God who created the world has indeed redeemed it in Christ, no task is more important than each of us growing up together in Christ. We do this by making promises to particular people, learning to forgive as we are forgiven, and trusting that there is enough grace to sustain us, even when we're not sure how it's all going to work out. Whether it's in a monastery, a community, a church, or a marriage, we make promises in hope that the God who made covenant with Abraham has made faithfulness possible for the whole world in Jesus. Our vows point to Jesus as a sign for the whole world: by grace we are being saved.

CHAPTER 5

Why It Matters Where We Live

TAKE THE ELEVATED TRAIN NORTH FROM PHILADELPHIA'S Center City and you soon find yourself in a post-industrial wasteland. Old factory buildings are surrounded by boarded up row-houses, interrupted by empty lots where plastic bags from corner stores roll like tumbleweeds. You might mistake some blocks here for a ghost town, except for the ceaseless noise that arises from the chaotic lives of people who are not so much ghosts as dead men walking—lives abandoned when everyone who could get out of this place did. The souls who were left to scrounge in these ruins eke out their existence from plastic wrappers and brown paper bags. Heroine has left so many of their eyes hollow that they mostly look down—or through you—when you pass them on the street. The train car rattles away overhead, stirring a wind at your back that brings with it the smell of urine mixed with dust. You have come to an abandoned place.

In the midst of this urban desert, on Norris Street, a sign hangs over a simple door proclaiming "New Jerusalem Now." Here the sidewalk is swept clean. If you follow it past the house you can see a garden in full bloom, flowers surrounding

Swiss chard and heirloom variety tomatoes, ripe on the vine. An inner-city oasis, this community is home to a couple of religious sisters and fifty recovering addicts. They begin their day with an hour of group Bible study, followed by household chores and two and half hours of community service. Members of the community feed their neighbors, tend the garden, run a small bio-diesel station, and offer Alternatives to Violence seminars. In the living room where they study Scripture together, a sign hangs on the wall: "My recovery will never be complete until I help to heal the society that made me sick."

For these brothers and sisters, healing begins on Norris Street. The new life they seek is not far away in a land they dream of, but right here in the abandoned place they call home. Though this street has been overlooked by city government, red-lined by lenders, avoided by real estate agents, and preyed on by hucksters, God is present. It's not just a feeling some people have here. You can see it. "I saw the Holy City, the new Jerusalem, coming down out of heaven from God," the apostle John writes in his Revelation 21:2. If you listen closely to the people who are finding new life at New Jerusalem Now, they echo the declaration that accompanied John's vision: "God's dwelling place is now among the people" (v. 3).

From the very beginning of the story of God's people, the promise of life with God is tied to a place on earth. God's promise to make Abraham into a great nation is not only a promise of children, but also of land. "I am the LORD, who brought you out of Ur of the Chaldeans to give you this land to take possession of it" (Genesis 15:7).

Conviction about promised land gives rise to the agony of

Israel's exile: "How can we sing the songs of the LORD while in a foreign land?" (Psalm 137:4). Relationship with God is so connected to relationship with the land that Israel cannot initially imagine worship in a new and foreign place. But this crisis of dislocation does not sever Israel's connection to place. It radically redefines it. "Seek the peace and prosperity of the city to which I have carried you into exile," God says through the prophet Jeremiah (29:7). Place matters, but Israel learns in Babylon that their God can hallow any ground. Indeed, "The earth is the Lord's and the fullness thereof; the world, and they that dwell therein" (Psalm 24:1 KJV). When we pay attention to our story, the centrality of our place on earth emerges as an essential element of what it means to be people of God's promise.

But we are not accustomed to being placed people. For all of the ways our story ties us to the ground from which we're made and the particular places where our God has met us, we also live in a culture of placelessness. We pride ourselves in being global citizens who know more about what's happening in New York and Tokyo than we know about the contours of the watershed in which we live and move and feed our children. While local culture may seem quaint (especially when we're on vacation), the ways and means of local places are not our standard models of success. The place we call home in a technological era is increasingly the bedroom community from which we connect by Internet or airplane with the people and issues that matter to us, wherever they happen to be.

Still, we long for home—for community, for roots, for a basic sense of belonging. No one knows this better than our marketing firms. A thousand times a day we are sold the experience of home. Whether it's in a car, a bank, or a cup of coffee, we are invited to buy a little bit of the stability that we can't seem to find in a culture where most of us are always on the go. But when the gift we were made for is reduced to a commodity, it cannot satisfy. A placeless culture threatens to hold us captive in the cyberspace of endless desire.

But God's desire for us is still more powerful. Scattered though we may be by the desires of our twisted selves, God insists on meeting us in the particularity of our daily lives. The chaos of a blighted neighborhood is interrupted by a New Jerusalem Now. The busy life of a contemporary churchgoer is confronted by words plainly spoken from a pastor tearing a piece of bread: "This is my body, broken for you." These signs are not the norm in our world, but neither are they an anomaly in the story of God's people. Concrete interruptions, they point to the peculiar way God is in the habit of breaking into a broken world.

"The Word became flesh and made his dwelling among us" (John 1:14).

Strange as it seems, God's incarnation in Jesus Christ is the fulfillment of the promise to Abraham and to Israel that God would make a home with us. God dwells with people in the particularity of our place and culture not so we can learn to transcend these particularities but so that we can know that our material lives have been redeemed. To stand with Jesus is to stand on holy ground.

The places where we live matter because we are, each of us, invited to participate in the mystery of Christ's incarnation. The New Testament calls the church the "body of Christ" because it assumes that Jesus' incarnation on the ground that was hallowed by his presence is extended into all the earth through the flesh and blood of people who have died to themselves and found new life by the Spirit. To live a life "in Christ" is to live in place, growing day by day into the fullness of the One who showed us how to engage our world faithfully. It is to pray not only with our words, but with our whole lives, "Thy kingdom come, thy will be done on earth as it is in heaven."

Standing on Holy Ground

Standard recovery wisdom says that if you want to change habits, you have to change people, places, and things. When addicts return to their old environment, they easily slip into old patterns. Programs that effectively relocate people have a lower relapse rate. Recovery is always a long road, but it usually begins by getting folks out of the mess they were in. For folks who are shackled by addiction, freedom often looks like leaving.

While this wisdom is certainly part of the program at New Jerusalem Now—everyone begins with a fifty day "black out" during which they have no contact with outsiders—this community's presence in North Philadelphia is enough of a contradiction to raise the question: Why would people serious about recovery decide to stay here? Why does this place matter?

Gary is a Lazarus. He inhabited the tombs of North Philadelphia for far more than three days, and he bore the stench to prove it. But over a decade ago, he was raised to new life at New Jerusalem Now. He helps to run the program now, a living testimony to folks who are just beginning that the dead are raised to life in this place. His presence raises the question that the Lord asked Ezekiel when he led him to an abandoned place, littered with dry bones: "Can these bones live?" (37:3).

Resurrection is the hope that Israel's prophets point to, anticipating Jesus not as a magic ball claims to know the future, but as a good composer knows where her song is going because everything points her in that direction. While a system of death lays claim to our lives and frustrates God's good creation, the constant hope of our story is that death does not have the last word. The same Spirit that hovered over the waters at creation can rattle bones together and cover tendons with flesh, restoring life to a glory that even exceeds its original goodness. This is what we see in the resurrection of Jesus, but it is already there in the prophet Ezekiel—already breaking forth in the lives of Lazarus and Gary. Ours is one story, start to finish.

If we pay attention to Ezekiel, however, we gain an appreciation for the way God's hope for us is tied to the land. In the chapter before the great valley of dry bones passage, the Lord instructs Ezekiel to prophesy concerning the land: "But you, mountains of Israel, will produce branches and fruit for my people, Israel, for they will soon come home. I am concerned for you and will look on you with favor; you will be plowed and sown" (36:8–9). These tender words of care are spoken as to a dearly beloved child. They are the song of a God who loves people and land alike, remembering that we are but dust that has been kissed by the eternal music.

But God's words are not directed toward soil in general; they are for the particular land that was promised to Abraham —the mountain from which Israel had been exiled when Ezekiel prophesied. This land is holy in a way that other places are not because God has promised to dwell among the people in this place. To understand how God saves us all through the one man, Jesus Christ, we have to internalize the peculiar logic of a God who blesses the whole world by calling one place holy.

Something about this rubs most of us the wrong way. We prefer a franchise model. If you want to reach the whole world with an idea or a product, common sense says that you start with something that can be easily replicated everywhere. Don't get too caught up in the details and local particularities. The franchise model says, "Focus on the big picture—on the things we all have in common." Cheap food that tastes good appeals to most people. Put a logo on that concept, and with some good marketing you can serve billions.

Why, then, does the God who "so loved the world" get all wrapped up in the particularities of Israel and their place rather than universalizing the principle of love? The answer, it seems, is tied up in the story that we have been given. "Salvation is of the Jews," Michael Wyschogrod writes, "because the flesh of Israel is the abode of the divine presence in the world. It is the carnal anchor that God has sunk into the soil of creation." While we might speculate about other possibilities, the only story we know about our Creator is one in which

Israel is the "carnal anchor" sunk deep in Palestine for the salvation of us all.

Incarnation, then, is not just about the second person of the Trinity becoming human. It is about Jesus getting born of a Jewish mother in Bethlehem of Judea. Our God does not offer a general and universal blessing on the world, but blesses the particular people of Israel in their particular place so that they can be a real blessing to all the nations of the earth. The good news that the church proclaims, then, is not a universalized spiritual message about our eternal status. It is, always, a particular invitation to become part of a placed people in the world.

We are not a franchise with billions served. We are a body rooted in Israel, called to hallow every place.

The church has struggled to internalize this from our very beginning. Paul, who began preaching the good news about Jesus in the synagogues of the Jewish Diaspora, struggled to articulate a gospel for all people that was, nevertheless, "first for the Jew, then for the Gentile" (Romans 2:10). What was manifestly clear from his experience, and later confirmed by the Jerusalem Council, was that God was moving to gather Jews and Gentiles into a new kind of community. This was the same God who had chosen to dwell among the people of Israel since Sinai. But this God's particular presence was manifest in a radically new way. The same Spirit that gave life to Jesus' body was now inhabiting the particular flesh of Jews and Gentiles in Jerusalem and Antioch, Ephesus and Corinth, Philippi and Rome. "Do you not know," Paul wrote to the early Christians living at Corinth, "that your bodies are temples of the Holy Spirit?" (1 Corinthians 6:19).

As living members of Christ's body in the world, the church existed in the particular places of the first century world as a temple, hosting God's presence and hallowing ground that had formerly been devoted to other gods (or simply viewed as real estate). When the blood of so many of those early saints was spilled out, they not only became martyrs in the church's memory. They, like Jesus, transformed the places where they worshiped and died. Their graves became holy ground, every bit as much as the temple mountain in Jerusalem.

Our resistance to God's way of engaging the world through particular people and places is not new. As the early church began to make sense of God's movement within the Greco-Roman world, its teachers recognized a tension between the deity philosophers imagined and the God who took on human flesh in Jesus. Many of the early heresies of the church —Gnosticism, Docetism, Arianism—were attempts to make Jesus a little more spiritual and a little less bound up in the messiness of matter and the particularity of Israel. What orthodoxy insisted on again and again, however, was that the Jewish man Jesus was in fact the Creator of the universe—the Word made flesh to dwell among us. Athanasius, who stood against the Arian heresy in the fourth century, wrote that the God who impressed the divine image on humanity in the beginning "secured this grace that He had given by making it conditional from the first upon two things—namely, a law and a *place*" (emphasis mine). The grace that was refused by

Adam and Eve *in Eden* was received by Abraham and Sarah *in Israel*. Though their faith was but the size of a mustard seed, it took root in such a way that salvation came to all the earth through their family *in Jesus*. From start to finish, grace is dependent on a place.

Jesus, then, is not just the promised son through whom all the world will be blessed; he is also, in his very Jewish flesh, the promised land that transforms every place. Early in John's gospel, Jesus makes a navigational decision that would have stood out to Jews of his day. Rather than walk around Samaria as good Jews had done since the time when Samaritans intermarried with their Assyrian occupiers, Jesus walks straight through Samaria. When he gets thirsty in the midst of enemy territory, Jesus sits down by a well and asks a Samaritan woman for a drink.

This woman is as surprised by Jesus as John's reader would have been, but in the course of their conversation, Jesus and the Samaritan woman get around to talking about their peoples' argument about place. " 'Sir,' the woman said, 'I can see that you are a prophet. Our ancestors worshiped on this mountain, but you Jews claim that the place where we must worship is in Jerusalem' " (John 4:19–20). Just a normal person on the street, this woman is attentive to her people's connection to place. She knows place has everything to do with worship. "Which is the true holy ground?" she is asking.

Jesus' answer is to the point: "A time is coming when you will worship the Father neither on this mountain nor in Jerusalem" (4:21). Clearly, this is a new day. Jesus' presence has radically altered the definition of holy ground. But Jesus has not come to break the promise of holy land; he is here to fulfill it. When Jesus says, "a time is coming and has now come when the true worshipers will worship the Father in spirit and in truth" (4:23), we are quick to focus on the spirit that floats above real places—on a divine principle that can now be applied in every place.

But the woman who has met Jesus is much closer to the truth of the ground. Remembering God's promises to Israel, she says, "I know that Messiah ... is coming. When he comes he will explain everything to us" (4:25). Jesus responds that he is Messiah—he is the One who has come to fulfill God's promises. Yes, God is spirit. But the Spirit that hovered over the ark of the covenant is now present in Jesus. God's Spirit has a carnal anchor in the world.

The argument between the Samaritans and the Jews was about the presence of God's Spirit in the ark. Both groups had a memory of possessing the ark in their place, yet after their return from exile, neither group could produce it. Neither could prove God's presence in the here and now. At this point in John's gospel, the Spirit has descended upon Jesus at his baptism, and Jesus has claimed to be the temple himself, telling the Pharisees in Jerusalem, "Destroy this temple, and I will raise it again in three days" (John 2:19). The signs of the story tell us what John declares in his prologue: the Word has become flesh and made his dwelling here among us.

Here in Samaria, with a woman at a well, Jesus makes clear how his incarnation redefines place. This woman is invited to worship God where she is—to see that she stands on holy ground—not because "God is everywhere" in an abstract sense, but because Jesus is *here* in the flesh. Wherever Jesus is standing with us, we can worship the Father in spirit and in truth. Wherever we stand "in Christ," we are to be about hallowing our place.

Engaging Our Place

Where we live matters because, as living members of Christ's body, our vocation is to make true worship possible in our place. This worship is not, as the woman at the well first assumed, confined to a house of worship. Gathering places are needed, and it is a great gift to have a room or building devoted to prayer. But church buildings do not define holy ground for those who are "in Christ." The ground we till to plant a garden, the streets connecting us one to another, the homes where we live, the shops where we work, the "third spaces" where we meet neighbors, the forests where nature's rhythms are preserved, the abandoned lot we overlook—all of these places are holy now. God wants to meet us here, and to meet our neighborhoods through us.

Monastic wisdom points us toward this understanding of being a placed people. The *monos* in monasticism is Greek for "one." From the very beginning of their life in the church, monks sought to focus their full attention on one thing. To pray without ceasing, to marry Christ, to worship God in spirit and in truth—this is the monastic vocation. It exists as a gift to all of us, as a concrete reminder that this is really all that any of us were made for. The whole point of human existence, as a later catechism taught us, is to "glorify God and enjoy Him forever."

If we pay attention to the monastic witness, its radical focus reveals something about how true worship compels people to engage our places. While monasticism began as a movement of solitary prayer in the desert, it quickly took on a communal expression. Pilgrims who found hospitality in the early desert communities brought their wisdom back to cities, integrating a vision for true worship into the life of the whole church. In Western monasticism, this wisdom was best summarized in Benedict of Nursia's *Rule*, a document that not only shaped monastic spirituality, but the life of Western civilization.

Giving themselves to the *Rule*'s pattern of *ora et labora* — "prayer and work" — Benedictine communities became anchors of society in Europe during the Middle Ages, offering stability and life-giving compassion to those around them through turmoils that were unimaginably chaotic by our contemporary standards. While critics have rightly observed that some Benedictines were corrupted by the power they amassed in Europe, their communities became a force in Western society while committed to nonviolence and gospel poverty. They grew both in number and influence not because they were eager to change the world but because they understood their vocation to be the worship of God in an authentic engagement with local places.

For the Benedictine, worship required Scripture study and prayer. But this commitment to the *opus Dei* — "the work of

God"—was always paired with a commitment to working the land and practicing the works of mercy. While the heritage of these communities includes beautiful manuscripts and time-honored prayer practices, we also have the Benedictines to thank for the modern university and hospital. Their work in education and healthcare instilled values in Western society that we all simply take for granted. Yet without the monastic witness, these institutions may well have never come to be.

To see the Benedictine witness as a sign pointing toward faithful engagement with our place is to see how true worship is always about prayer and work—an inward journey and an outward journey. Most of what Christians do in our worship gatherings is about inner work. We pray and study, fellowship and praise. But the work we do outside of these gatherings is also worship. When we care for our children or organize our neighborhoods; when we teach and care for the sick; when we welcome the stranger and feed the hungry; when we conduct business for the common good and create beautiful art—all of this is worship too. To find our rhythm as a people who gather to pray and go out to work, all as a life or worship, is to learn what it means to see our place as holy ground.

In the history of the church, this way of understanding worship was wrapped up in the parish system. Strongly influenced by the Benedictine witness, Christians in the West understood themselves for centuries as members of the church universal in a particular parish. Church-shopping would not have made any sense to these people. The congregation you belonged to was determined by the zip code where you lived. You were a member of your parish. This meant that the worship gathering of your faith community was in walking distance of your home. When you gathered with brothers and sisters in Christ, you were gathering with your physical neighbors. In our contemporary language, everyone was a member of a neighborhood church.

In this system, the vocation of the church to engage its particular place was clear. *How* particular individuals and groups engaged their place varied, of course. But that you were called to engage your village or neighborhood as a member of Christ's body was simply assumed.

Even before this understanding of place was disrupted by modern technologies of mobility, it was fragmented by divisions within the church. When Catholics and Protestants could no longer worship together, one group ran the other out of town—or, after they had agreed not to kill one another, they set up two different parishes in the same place. The multiplication of denominational divisions that followed coincided with the rise of a consumer culture, resulting in a contemporary context where congregations compete for members but are not sure how to help the people they attract to engage the places where they live.

For so many of us today, church is a place where you go on Sunday, just like work or school or home are the places we go every other day of the week. Where we live often has little to do with where we worship. This makes it difficult to see how we're called to make our whole life true worship in a place.

But incarnation interrupts us. To confess that Jesus took on flesh and moved into the neighborhood is to see that we are invited to dwell in our places and grow up into "the fullness of him who fills everything in every way" (Ephesians 1:23). As the letter to the church at Ephesus demonstrates so well, the power of God that raised Jesus from the dead is within us to overcome the "principalities and powers" (6:12) of our present age. A culture of hyper-mobility is not greater than God's plan to redeem the world through Christ's body, the church. But Ephesians is equally clear that this power is made manifest in the peculiar way of engagement that we learn from Israel and Jesus: "our struggle is not against flesh and blood, but ... against the spiritual forces of evil in the heavenly realms. Therefore, put on the full armor of God, so that ... you may be able to stand your ground" (6:12 – 13).

If we pay attention to the conquest stories of Israel, we learn that God's people did not gain their promised land through cunning or military might. They left Egypt through the Red Sea because God made a way out of no way. When they came to Jericho, it was God who made the walls come tumbling down. Israel's greatest hero, David, won his monumental battle against the Philistine giant, Goliath, by refusing the royal armor and trusting God to use the simple slingshot he carried as a shepherd boy. Over and again, God makes clear that Israel isn't in charge of securing its own place in the world. "The LORD will fight for you," Moses says; "you need only to be still" (Exodus 14:14).

This standing in place is the posture that the New Testament exhorts the church to maintain. Jesus told Peter, the rock upon whom he promised to build his church, that he should put away his sword in the garden of Gethsemane. The violence of this world's kingdoms would not be the means by which God would establish the peaceable kingdom here on earth. Jesus' refusal of worldly power is not, however, a passive submission to the status quo. Jesus stands before Pilate, just as the martyrs would stand before authorities after him, neither backing down nor succumbing to the ways of an order that is passing away. "Fight the good fight of the faith," Paul exhorted his young disciple, Timothy (6:12), recalling that Timothy had made the same "good confession" Jesus made while testifying before Pontius Pilate. It was a confession made not so much with his mouth as with his feet. In the power of the Spirit, he stood his ground.

The recovering addicts at New Jerusalem Now in North Philadelphia cannot imagine their own redemption apart from the redemption of their place. They know in their bones that they must be born again; they know just as surely that they need new homes and new businesses, new manners and new friends, new food and new fun, a new heaven and a new earth. It is striking, though, that even as they are giving their whole selves to building a new society in the shell of the old, they are equally committed to unlearning the habits of power and control that those who are apparently successful in our society often assume. Their Alternatives to Violence seminars, alongside their vigils against war and capital punishment, testify to the way they are learning to "fight the good fight of the faith." To pay attention to their witness is to see how the transformation of our own places depends on learning the peculiar way of standing that we see in the stories of Israel and Jesus.

Hope for a Future

Our vocation to stand in the places where we live and see the salvation of the Lord is not only a declaration that God is with us here and now; it is also a proclamation that our broken dwelling places have a future. This conviction is right there in the name of New Jerusalem Now. Their present is being transformed by what has been promised for the future.

Eschatology is the traditional name for teaching about the "last things"—the end toward which our whole story points us. The last book in our Bible is Revelation, where John writes about his vision of the New Jerusalem, descending from heaven down to earth. It is an apocalyptic book, filled with signs and symbols that have been interpreted in myriad ways through the centuries. But to see Revelation as the culmination of the biblical narrative is to see how its symbols draw on the long story of God's relationship with Israel. A New Jerusalem matters, after all, only if you know the promise of this city of peace.

When the people of Israel heard Ezekiel prophesy to the mountains, they thought first of all about the mountain of mountains—their beautiful city of Zion, Jerusalem. About this city Isaiah prophesied, "Your gates will always stand open, they will never be shut day or night, so that people may bring you the wealth of the nations" (60:11). This capital city of the promised land, destroyed though it was during exile, was to be rebuilt as a beacon of light for the whole world. Isaiah again, exhorting the city itself: "Arise, shine, for your light has come, and the glory of the LORD rises upon you"

(61:1). All the hope that God has invested in Israel is focused on their city, Jerusalem. So the psalmist teaches the people to sing, "I lift up my eyes to the mountains—where does my help come from? My help comes from the LORD, the Maker of heaven and earth" (Psalm 121:1).

This great hope for God's holy mountain, Jerusalem, is in the background for those who hear Jesus when he goes up on one of Palestine's smaller mounts and says to the crowd, "You are the light of the world. A town built on a hill cannot be hidden." The "town" in Matthew's Greek is *polis*, from which we get our English word *politics*. The message Jesus came preaching is political to the extent that it intends to bring people together in particular places to share a distinctive way of life, which is good news to all people. What New Jerusalem Now says about recovery is true for all of us: our healing cannot be complete until our places are made new in Christ.

In the twentieth century, the political vision of God's people as a "holy hill" energized both the progressive social-gospel movement and the more conservative Religious Right. Though often seen as opposing forces by Christians in America, these two political movements had in common the conviction that the technologies and political apparatus of modern America could be employed by well-meaning people to bring salvation to the whole world. Whether that meant ending war or ending abortion, the message was the same: if we work hard enough, we can fight back the devil and establish God's city here on earth.

The failure of both of these movements is, in some ways, a basic lesson in eschatology. While our faith is, indeed, "this worldly" and the Bible offers a political vision from start to finish, we are not responsible for establishing Jerusalem by our own might. "Unless the Lord builds the house, its builders labor in vain," the psalmist teaches us to sing as we make our way up the mountain to Jerusalem. "Unless the Lord watches over the city, the watchmen stand guard in vain" (Psalm 127:1). If we pay attention to the prophets, they tell Israel over and again that her attempts to secure Jerusalem through alliance with worldly powers is idolatry. "Woe to those who go down to Egypt for help," Isaiah declares, "who rely on horses, who trust in the multitude of their chariots" (31:1). Likewise, when Jesus is making his way up to Jerusalem, he teaches the disciples a distinctive way of political engagement: "You know that the rulers of the Gentiles lord it over them, and their high officials exercise authority over them. Not so with you. Instead, whoever wants to become great among you must be your servant, and whoever wants to be first must be your slave" (Matthew 20:25–27).

That we ascend by descending is a basic insight of monastic spirituality in the Christian East and West. Both Benedict, who introduces the ladder of humility in his *Rule*, and John Climacus, who wrote *The Ladder of Divine Ascent*, the most popular spiritual guide in the East for over a thousand years, say more or less the same thing: "As he who climbs up a rotten ladder runs a risk, so all honor, glory, and authority oppose humility and bring down him who has them."[8] God's way up is down—all the way down to the dirt beneath our feet. We engage our place in the way of Jesus when we humbly serve the people and the land God has given us right where we are.

"We can do no great things," Mother Teresa often said, "only small things with great love." To confess this with the saints is not to give up on the glorious political vision of the New Jerusalem, but rather to trust that what the Revelation says about Jesus is true: he is, indeed, the Alpha and the Omega, the beginning and the end. The very One who made us has put on flesh and dwelt among us so that we might see in his death and resurrection the end toward which his is leading us. More than anything else, eschatology teaches us to see that the end of our story has interrupted us in the middle. We do not have to worry whether God's way will win out in the end. Jesus stands victorious in the present.

A couple of years ago, Sister Margaret planned to retire from her work at New Jerusalem Now. Entering her ninth decade of life, she thought it was time to hand over some of the responsibilities she bore as founder of her community and watch a new generation take the lead. In keeping with her hope for local redemption, she was glad to pass her leadership position on to a native of the place who had come through the program. The transition went well for several months until the new leader was overcome by temptation and ran off with all the money he had access to. It was a huge blow to the community, almost enough to close their doors.

But somehow they kept going. Grace came in new friends and unexpected gifts. Sister Margaret was not able to retire but found strength for a new season in the same vision that had sustained her up until then. "My journey through all these twists and turns has been in one consistent direction," she wrote years before this crisis: "away from the distortions in my heart caused by the spirit of Empire and towards God and the New Jerusalem."⁹ To make this journey from Egypt's death system to the new life of Jerusalem is the vocation of every person made in God's image. To make it with others, in the particular place where we live, is to learn how we have been caught up in God's reconciliation of all things.

CHAPTER 6

Why We Live Together

ON A COLD AND CLEAR DECEMBER AFTERNOON, I CATCH A ride with a friend from Chicago to the Reba Place Fellowship in Evanston, Illinois. Though Reba has been here for nearly fifty years, this is my local friend's first visit—and mine too. "Reba Place," which is a cross street lined with trees and sidewalks, is easy enough to find. The address I have is for a basement office where some of the fellowship's nonprofit ministries are managed. There I meet David, a dear soul whom I know from Christian community gatherings elsewhere. We greet one another, and he is eager to show me around his neighborhood. We pull on our winter hats and head out for a walk.

You don't have to go far in this neighborhood to meet someone who is associated with the Reba Place Fellowship. Within a few blocks we pass a church building, a gathering place, a day care, dozens of houses and apartment buildings, all somehow related to this network of people. It's hard to know just how to count them (the people, that is). The fellowship has covenanted members and novice members, as well as an apprentice house for young people who are checking things out. Some seventy people fit into one of those categories, but their lives also intersect with a local Mennonite congregation of several hundred (also called Reba Place) and dozens of neighbors who live in low-income housing that the fellowship owns. As we walk along the sidewalks that connect these people and their places, I meet folks who are more than neighbors. In a palpable way, they belong to one another. I get their stories in pieces as we walk along and begin to try and fit them together.

A couple of hours later, I am sitting in a living room, listening to a woman in her sixties recount a disagreement she had with another member of the community this week. Just to hear it, I'd say it was a relatively minor misunderstanding. But clearly there is more than I can hear. "I was angry," she says matter-of-factly, and I notice the tears forming in the corners of her eyes. Her anger has a history, tied up in ways that I cannot understand with an intimate and complex relationship that has developed over decades. "I knew that I had to go and talk to her," she says. "Because community isn't possible without forgiveness."

A few years later, I am on the sidewalks of Reba Place again, this time to celebrate the fiftieth anniversary of the fellowship. Over six hundred people have come, each with their own piece of this community's story. Some recall the early days, in the late 1950s, when a couple of families decided to try to live out the communal vision of the early church in Acts. By every account, it was harder than they imagined. More than once, it almost fell apart. But in the 1970s, when the community experienced a charismatic renewal and the

Jesus People movement had lots of Christians talking about community, this group swelled in size and influence. An exciting season for many, it was also a painful time. I think back to that evening in the living room, on my first visit here, and the woman's testimony about both the difficulty and the necessity of forgiveness. For some who are here now, this is their first time back in twenty or thirty years. They have come because, despite the pain, they learned something here that they haven't forgotten: our journey toward God is a journey that draws us closer to one another.

From the very beginning of the story the Bible tells, life together with other people is imaged as an essential part of life with God. Family plays such an essential role in Judaism because, for people who know the creation story of Genesis, the most basic unit of human community is the two who become "one flesh" in marriage. This form of life together is instituted before the Fall — before sin ever entered into the world — and continues as a form through which redemption is made possible in Israel. The marriage of Abraham and Sarah is the context in which Israel learns what faith means. When God calls these two to be the parents of God's people, he first calls them to be parents.

But even here, in the first family of God's people, we learn something about the challenge of human community in a world that is twisted by sin. Abraham and Sarah want to trust God, but they simply can't see how they'll ever become the parents of a great nation if, going into their nineties, they still don't have a son. They have failed to trust the Creator's power that John the Baptist will later proclaim: "Out of these stones God can raise up children of Abraham" (Matthew 3:9). A life together as God's holy people is not an accomplishment that we achieve through cunning. It is a gift from our Creator. The challenge is to learn to live in the way of that gift.

The scandal of Jesus is a scandal of grace. With regard to the family of Israel, it is a twofold scandal. First sign that Jesus has come to redefine God's people: he doesn't marry. The first commandment was and always had been, "Be fruitful and multiply." Children of Israel could not imagine how this was possible apart from men and women marrying to establish families. Yet Jesus emerges on the public scene as a thirty year-old single man to say, "The kingdom of God is at hand." God has drawn near, and the divine order is disrupting the status quo of Jewish society.

Which brings us to the second sign that Jesus offers a new interpretation of what it means to be part of God's holy people: he throws the gates open to outsiders. Jesus' choice of the single life begs the question, "How then is God going to raise up a new generation of people?" Jesus' answer comes in his radical hospitality toward those who had been counted out. "I have other sheep that are not of this sheep pen. I must bring them also" (John 10:16).

In Luke's gospel, this claim that God is inviting the outsiders to come in—that, in fact, they're rushing in ahead of the rightful heirs—is what nearly gets Jesus killed before he ever leaves his hometown. And while his claim to be God is ultimately what sends Jesus to the cross, that claim of divine authority is the grounds upon which he is bold to assert a new imagination for life together among God's people. Jesus redefines family values, insisting that our life together is both radically dependent on God's providence and radically open to the outsider whom God might invite in.

This grace-dependent and graciously hospitable understanding of fellowship—what the New Testament calls *koinonia*—is what animates the movement of early Christianity. At Antioch, the converted rabbi Paul sees that God's Spirit has fallen upon Jews and Gentiles alike, making them brothers and sisters in the same family. From that point on, he understands his mission to be the proclamation of this gospel to the whole world: "The Gentiles are heirs together with Israel, members together of one body, and sharers together in the promise in Christ Jesus" (Ephesians 3:6). In Jesus, we learn to call Abraham and Sarah our parents and to call one another "sister" and "brother." Suddenly, we have family where before we had strangers and enemies. This is a whole new world.

This understanding of the family of God does not translate easily into a society that prizes the rights of the individual. Suspicious of the ways that traditional family and social structures abused the weak and oppressed minorities, modern people have worked hard to protect the autonomy and freedom of the individual over and against the coercion of others. As a U.S. Supreme Court Justice famously put it, "Your rights end where the tip of my nose begins." A rights-based society, then, frees us to do what we want to so long as we're not hurting anyone else.

But subject as we are to the disease of original sin, we are not happy when we get to do what we want. Indeed, we not only end up infringing on others; we hurt ourselves. So it is that a society that prizes individual rights must have an abundance of lawyers and therapists. We litigate our poor relationships and analyze our neurotic habits, hoping to find a way out of the bondage that our freedom affords us. But in all of this, we end up feeling rather lonely.

The deepest hunger of a radically autonomous society is the longing for community. The stories we tell ourselves at the movies suggest that this longing will be fulfilled when we find "the one"—the perfect end of every romance story. Marketing gurus tell us in ten thousand ads a day that our deep need for belonging will be met by purchasing the products that the community we want to be part of purchases. The restlessness of our modern soul is manifest in a fascination with all things communal (online communities, planned communities, community investments, community-supported agriculture ...) coupled with a decreased capacity to commit to any particular group of people. As a society we are community starved without any collective capacity to prioritize the common good.

Thus, the *koinonia* of the New Testament is both fascinating and frightening to most of us. We would love to believe that the witness of a community like Reba Place Fellowship points toward a different way of life that is possible for both singles and married people—a community that we could be part of, over a lifetime, in the places where we live. And at the same time, a community like this scares us to death. What keeps it from turning into a cult? Who decides when someone gets to leave? And what can you take with you when you leave if members share property in common?

It's worth noting that the fears that come up when we think about a community like Reba Place are not unlike the fears that keep people from getting married, joining a congregation, or even staying in the same neighborhood. When we open ourselves up to other people, things inevitably get messy. Marriages fail, congregations have power struggles, and neighborhoods change. How could anyone commit to other people in a world so full of uncertainty?

While this crisis of commitment may seem like a sign of our times, it is deeply rooted in the anxiety of membership that all of creation has been subject to since the Fall. Christians believe that Jesus died and rose again to redeem us from this anxiety. "For he himself is our peace," the letter to the Ephesians says, "who has ... destroyed the barrier, the dividing wall of hostility" (2:14). Whether in marriage, congregational life, intentional or monastic community, Christians live together in the hope that our deepest longings are fulfilled in the community of sisters and brothers to whom we are reconciled even as we are reconciled to God in Christ.

The desert father Dorotheus of Gaza offers a striking image for this hope. Imagine, he says, a huge circle on which all people are standing on the circumference, looking in. Now, imagine the point at the center of that circle as the place where God is. If you draw a line from each person to where God is, and if you imagine each person moving along that line toward God, you can also see each of us drawing closer to one another. This, Dorotheus said, is why Jesus said the greatest commandment is to "love the Lord your God with all your heart and with all your soul and with all your mind and with all your strength," and the second is like it: "love your neighbor as yourself"' (Mark 12:30–31). Because both loves move us in the same direction.

The Ship of Faith

On my first visit to Reba Place, that cold December weekend, I met a young man named Eric who told me his story. The son of parents who divorced about the time he was hitting puberty, Eric entered the rebellion of adolescence with an extra dose of anger toward the authority figures in his life. Rage against the Machine became his soundtrack, and he relished in the adrenaline rush that came with attacking the evils of imperialism, capitalism, pseudo-democracy, and conventional morality. Intelligent and intense, he saw through the hypocrisy of the society around him and longed to find an authentic way to live, free from the artificiality of mainstream American life. In his early twenties, somewhere between WTO protests and antiwar rallies, he heard about the Reba Place Fellowship. This group caught his attention because they didn't buy into the American Dream, and they weren't just sitting up late on the weekends talking about it. They were living an alternative, seven days a week.

His dreadlocks pulled back in a pony-tail, Eric's eyes are unobscured. They are soft, and I can see that the anger he's been describing is no longer burning behind them. Unashamed, he looks at me and says, "The people here have helped me to heal." What they've given him is pure gift, and he knows it. He smiles like a man rescued from a burning building.

In the early church, when Christianity was a persecuted minority movement within the Roman Empire, one of the main images that Christian teachers used to describe the fellowship of believers was a ship on a storm-tossed sea. As in the time of Noah, they said, God's good creation was subject to a flood of powers. False gods demanded allegiance, called for sacrifice, and promised a happy life to those who would renounce Jesus and bow to them. Yet, with the eyes of faith, Christians could see that the apparent success and comfort of mainstream society was ultimately a mirage. The Roman world and its systems of power were passing away.

These early Christian teachers remembered what Jesus had said: "As it was in the days of Noah, so it will be at the coming of the Son of Man. For in the days before the flood, people were eating and drinking, marrying and giving in marriage, up to the day Noah entered the ark; and they knew nothing about what would happen until the flood came" (Matthew 24:37–39). Because they remembered Jesus as the "Son of Man" who walked among them, died, and rose again, these early Christians did not recall this as a prediction about the future but as a description of the historical events they had witnessed in the birth of the Christian movement. God had, indeed, provided a ship of faith to carry them through the storm. Their name for that vessel was "church."

Ecclesiology is the name that tradition assigns to teaching about the nature and purpose of the church. Literally the "reasons for the gathering," ecclesiology attempts to make sense of why we live together. It takes as its starting point that the God who called Noah into the ark now calls people from every tribe, tongue, and nation into the ship of faith called "church." What the early Christians saw, and ecclesiology has always affirmed, is that the main purpose of this gathering is salvation. To be without a ship when the waters rise is to be swept away by the powers of death and destruction. But to hear the call to get on board this ship is, literally, to be saved. The early church had a summary statement for this conviction: "Without the church there is no salvation."

To recall this shorthand in our own time is to raise a host of questions about who is "in" and who is "out" in God's story. From our perspective, this bit of doctrine sounds narrow-minded and exclusive. Does it imply that only Christians know the wisdom of God in the present and have the hope of eternal life in the future? What about someone like Gandhi who was manifestly better at doing the things Jesus did and taught than most people who claim to follow Jesus? Was his life really less abundant than the Christian missionaries who tried to convert him? Is he now burning in hell while they experience eternal bliss? Such exclusivity is hard to swallow for people who have seen signs of real life outside the church.

What is more, we have also seen those who gather in Jesus' name commit terrible atrocities. From the Crusades and the Inquisition of the Middle Ages to the Holocaust and contemporary sex-abuse scandals, Christian history makes it difficult to distinguish those who are being saved from those who are ensnared in this world's system of death. If an outsider like Gandhi can be better than the average Christian and, at the same time, the average congregation can be worse than the world around it, what sense does it make to claim that the church is God's vehicle for salvation in the world?

When faced with questions like these, it helps that the church has Israel's history to learn from. If we pay attention to the story of God's people, it quickly becomes clear that while they were called to be set apart, Israel was chronically bad at living up to the holiness God gave them as their standard. This is why they wandered as a people in the wilderness for forty years before God allowed them to enter into the Promised Land. It is, again, why they went through a cycle under their judges of listening to God, then straying away, then facing judgment, only to return again to the God who had called them. When Israel asked to have a king like other nations, the prophet Samuel told them it was a bad idea. Before, during, and after Israel's exile from the Promised Land, prophets repeated this theme. Israel's only hope of salvation was to trust the true and living God. When they failed to do this, God used outsiders to show Israel what faithfulness looked like.

Take King Nebuchadnezzar, for example. Ruler of the Babylonians, Nebuchadnezzar was enemy number one of Israel. In 597 BCE, his forces defeated Jerusalem and sent the first set of exiles in chains to Babylon. Among them was Daniel, a young man who insisted, against all evidence, that what his people had always believed was still true—their only hope was faithful obedience to the God who called them his own. While the prophet Jeremiah insisted that exile was God's judgment, not God's defeat, Daniel put this faith into practice. As a remnant in Israel and the church always has, Daniel trusted God's way in the midst of Babylon. But he also recorded the testimony of the most unlikely witness to God's power. Nebuchadnezzar himself, after resisting Daniel's God, saw the light and confessed, "I, Nebuchadnezzar, praise and exalt and glorify the King of heaven, because everything he does is right and all of his ways are just. And those who walk in pride he is able to humble" (Daniel 4:37). The King who testifies to the truth about God in the book of Daniel is the enemy king, Nebuchadnezzar.

When Israel fails to be faithful, God sends an enemy to humble them, only to then humble the enemy and make him a witness to God's power. In Israel, through Israel, and even despite Israel, God is working out a plan to redeem the whole universe. The point isn't that Israel is more holy than other nations. The point is that Israel's God is King of the universe.

"Without the church there is no salvation" is not, then, a claim that God's people "get it" while everyone else is missing the point. When Jesus shows up in the first century, it is not Israel's King Herod or his scribes who recognize the long awaited Messiah, but rather "magi from the East"—foreign kings who, once again, see more clearly than those who think they are "in." What was true of Israel is true of the church: our leaders miss the point, we can (as a group) be further from God's kingdom than our non-Christian neighbors, and magi like Gandhi who come to Jesus with fresh eyes often see him more clearly than we do. All of this is true, and still we confess: *Outside the church there is no salvation.*

Why? Because salvation does not depend on the performance of the called. Salvation depends on the God who calls us. And the only story we know is a story in which we're called to live together as God's gathered people.

"Think of what you were when you were called," Paul says to the church in Corinth. "Not many of you were wise by human standards; not many were influential; not many were of noble birth. But God chose the foolish things of the world to shame the wise; God chose the lowly things of this world— and the despised things. . . . It is because of him that you are in Christ Jesus" (1:27 – 30). Even before the church's embarrassing history of excesses and abuses, Paul knew that we were not an exceptional bunch. This did not in the slightest sense lower his expectation for what God was doing through the church. And yet, at the very same time, Paul pointed out how the life together that we are called to reveals our weakness —our inability, even—to live together peaceably in a world that is falling apart (when the Corinthians gathered to eat together at the Lord's table, some of them went hungry while others got drunk). How can such a messy life together be the very context of our salvation?

Because these are the relationships in which we learn what it means to be in Christ. The God whom we know in Jesus is here, as always, the God who exists eternally as Father, Son, and Holy Spirit. If the doctrine of the incarnation helps us to see that it was the eternal Son who died, rose, and ascended into heaven, where he is seated at the right hand of the Father, then ecclesiology pushes us to understand how the same Spirit who gave life to the body of Jesus in the incarnation is now giving life to the body called church. "And if the Spirit of him who raised Jesus from the dead is living in you," Paul writes to the Romans, "he who raised Christ from the dead will also give life to your mortal bodies because of his Spirit who lives in you" (8:11).

I don't think it an accident of history that Reba Place Fellowship, after a decade of trying to share life together as an intense, seven-days-a-week, share-everything-in-common expression of church, experienced a charismatic renewal. When they heard the call to follow Jesus with their whole lives, they heard a call to live together. And yet, in the intimacy and intensity of that life together, they quickly experienced the messy and painful reality—the impossible possibility— of church. While the nature of our life together in Christ's body does not always look like an intentional Christian community, the intensity of a place like Reba Place Fellowship makes clear what ecclesiology says is true for all believers: our life together is radically dependent on the power of the Spirit to raise us from the dead.

In our congregational and family lives, as at Reba Place and Corinth and Rome, this resurrection happens in the context of relationships. Left to our own will, we wander like the young man, Eric, able to see all that is wrong in the systems and people around us, yet slaves to the same will that tells us we don't want *that*, but something better. God calls us into life with other people so that we can learn how the problems we see "out there" are also in us. The world is a mess because we are a mess. But in Christ, a love is possible in the face of our mess. "While we were still sinners, Christ died for us"

(Romans 5:8). While we are yet sinners, Christians love one another in Christ.

What was true for Eric can be true for all of us: love in community heals us, raises us from the dead, even, to know the power of new life in Christ. One of the founders of Reba Place Fellowship, John Miller, wrote, "The Christian church has no other purpose in this world than to extend the mission of Jesus by establishing communities of love." Each one a lifeboat, such communities attract people who are dying and do not know it. When we come face-to-face with ourselves in another, we cannot hide from our own mess. But when we are loved with Christ's love, something new is born within us. This is the resurrection life we find on the ship of faith into which we're all invited.

It's no accident that the folks at Reba call their preschool "Little Ark." They've learned that the whole point of life together is to send out little arks of love into the world.

Love as Our True Work

While most people know, deep down somewhere, that we are created for love and that our deepest wounds cannot be healed apart from it, the fact of the matter is that most people have to get up and go to work most days. Spiritual needs are relegated to Sundays (or, for the spiritually robust, Sundays *and* Wednesday nights). Healing has its place in the therapist's office or on a retreat or in those hard conversations that we have late at night in the kitchen, when we know we're stealing time from sleep. Individuals in a busy world, we get our love in where we can. But we learn to be realistic. There's work to be done, so we keep moving.

When we're most hopeful—often when we're in school, *before* we've launched into the day-to-day practicalities of a career—we talk about our work as a vocation. At the root of that word *vocation* is the Latin equivalent of the Greek *kaleo*, the root that signifies this notion of church we've been considering. Both roots mean the same thing: "to call." We talk about being "called" to a particular job in our society because of the influence of the Protestant Reformation. In Europe during the Middle Ages, a sort of hierarchy developed between ordained ministers who served the church and lay members of the church who farmed the land and built houses and made shoes. In most people's minds, religious work was a calling from God—a vocation—while everything else was just work to be done. This distinction created a sort of two-tiered church of upper- and lower-class Christians.

When the Protestant Reformation (and the Roman Catholic Counter-Reformation) sought to amend this unhealthy division within Christendom, it did so by declaring that all work is a calling. The cobbler in his shoe shop may cobble to the glory of God every bit as much as the monk in his cell or the priest in the parish does his work to that end. Everything is holy now, so anyone can be a priest (the Protestants called this doctrine the "priesthood of all believers"). The hierarchy between clergy and laity has been eliminated. While the distinction remains, it marks a difference in roles, not in importance (thus the pope, though the highest of priests, is called "servant of servants.")

As a word for the church, this is good news indeed. But over the centuries, as it combined with the secularizing forces of the modern world and the resultant individualism of Western society, this notion of vocation came to mean something else. "Your work is your calling" has meant more and more that the most important thing in most people's lives is our job. So we make decisions about education based on job potential. We choose where we live based on job availability. And we see new job opportunities as a legitimate reason to uproot our families and leave our communities.

What began, then, as corrective language within the church has become a notion in society that makes life together difficult for the church. Most of us just assume that the most important work we have to do in the world is the nursing we do at the hospital, the teaching we do at a school, the administrating we do at a government office, or the business we do at a corporation. At our most idealistic, we imagine that this work is the contribution we make to the sustenance and betterment of society. And at our most cynical we say that, like it or not, it's how we pay the bills. But whatever our mood, the assumption remains: our job is our true work and calling.

Ecclesiology matters because it teaches us to see how church challenges this most common of assumptions. We are not, primarily, called to be doctors or lawyers, janitors or mechanics. We are called to be living members of Christ's body in the world. Do we still work as doctors and lawyers, janitors and mechanics? Yes. But this is not who we are. Our income earning work is not what defines us. It doesn't determine who we belong to. It's not even our most important work.

Our most important work is love.

We live together so we can put love into practice.

The people who loved Eric back to health at Reba Place are secretaries and contractors, college professors and social workers. They go to work at the office or the job site most days, and they do their work well. But they are a church — they share a life together in Jesus' name — so they can do the more important work that Jesus called them to when he said, "As I have loved you, so you must love one another" (John 13:34). They are able to offer Eric the healing love of Jesus because they have received it from one another, day after day, in this place. Though it is not easy, that love has become a habit of being, put to practice in concrete acts of forgiveness. To be with them is to know that they have found the work that all of us are made for.

We live together, then, to realize our true vocation in Christ. For some people, this life together as church takes the form of intentional or monastic community. In a promise of obedience to fellow sisters and brothers, they learn what it means to die to themselves and be born again in the pursuit of unity for the greater good. A Benedictine monk once told me the story of going to visit his brother and sister-in-law for a weekend after living at the monastery for nearly twenty years. Watching this couple manage a home with several kids, juggling schedules to meet everyone's needs, the monk said, "I made a vow of obedience, but now I see what it really means." For most Christians, family is the context where we learn to do the true work of love.

"The wife does not have authority over her own body but

yields it to her husband," Paul writes, describing Christian marriage to the Corinthians. "In the same way, the husband does not have authority over his own body but yields it to his wife" (1 Corinthians 7:4). To be married, then, is to begin to know what it means that we are not our own. We belong to another. But our mutual belonging in the community of marriage also opens us up to hospitality. When a couple starts a home together, they create a space where sisters and brothers can gather and where strangers can be welcomed, as our Lord insisted they should be. When husband and wife give their bodies to one another, one of the strangest guests they often welcome is a child. As the monk observed in his brother's home, this is their opportunity to practice obedience. Giving themselves for the sake of another, they learn the abundant life that Jesus taught and practiced.

But to practice family life in our fragmented society is to feel in our gut how much we need a broader community — an extended family of people who are willing to love us and lay down their lives for us when we have, as individuals, simply come to the end of our rope. Every young couple knows that a long weekend with family or friends is often the thing that saves a marriage, just as, the regular help that we get from friends, neighbors, and grandparents is often just enough to get us through to the end of another week. Yet, in a society where education and work often removes us from the extended biological family for whom such help is natural, families often don't make it. Though divorce rates have gone down slightly over the past decade, half of first marriages still fall apart—and the percentages go up sharply for subsequent marriages.

In view of this social reality, the New Testament's image of the church as the family of God is more radical than it may have first seemed. For in a world where extended families have been scattered and nuclear families are floundering, the church promises to be a family where people from every tongue, tribe, and nation share life together in the places where we are as members of one body. In a world where so many people are homeless, both materially and spiritually, Jesus' promise sounds like good news: "Where you had a home, you will have homes."

We live together, in the end, because we have been called to be good news for the whole world. As families, communities, and congregations, our work is to put true love into practice so neighbors can see with their eyes—right here on a street like Reba Place—that we have been saved.

CHAPTER 7

Why We Would
Rather Die Than Kill

I am sitting in the lobby of a small hotel in Baghdad, listening to an American grandmother who has spent her last six months in Iraq. She is a member of the Christian Peacemaker Teams (CPT), a literal reserves for foot soldiers in the army of the Lord. Since 1986, CPT has made it their mission to "get in the way" of violence by practicing direct action non-violence in conflict zones. I grew up singing camp songs about being in the Lord's army, but never imagined the call of duty would lead me here. I am in a war zone, my head foggy from several nights of interrupted sleep, looking to a wiser soul for direction.

She is frank, but not alarming. Many of CPT's Iraqi friends are suggesting that we leave. Saddam Hussein's regime is crumbling, the city is under siege, and every night brings another series of bombs that shake the earth beneath us. We have been eager to know what we can do, but the locals know too well how little can be done when every night is spent hunkered down with the kids, listening to air-raid sirens, and waiting to see if the roof comes crashing in on you. Why be here if you don't have to be—if it's not your home, your kids, your city that you're praying will be spared from this madness?

In the distance, somewhere out on the city's edge, we hear bombing begin again. This brings a pause to the morning report, and I look around this circle of twenty peacemakers to gauge the general level of anxiety. An older gentleman across from me, his hands crossed on his lap, has his face turned up to the sky from which the bombs are falling. He begins to sing:

> Over my head, I hear music in the air.
> Over my head, I hear music in the air.
> Over my head, I hear music in the air.
> There must be a God somewhere.

I remember a few days ago hearing a reporter ask this man if he was afraid. "Oh, yes, I'm afraid," he said calmly. Then, with a slight smile, he added, "But maybe not for the reason you think. I'm not afraid of dying. My life belongs to God. But I am afraid of the belief that war brings freedom. I am afraid to sit at home while this kind of violence is carried out by my government. I am afraid that what Martin Luther King said is true: our only choice now is between nonviolence and nonexistence."

We decide to stay, at least for the time being, and we survive the bombing. A couple of days later, I go home as siege turns to occupation and terrorist cells spring up with the single mission of driving out US troops by any means necessary. CPT stays to accompany Iraqis through check-points manned by teenagers from the Midwest, to inquire about accusations of abuse at prisons, to train a Muslim Peacemaker Team, to say over and again, "Another way is possible."

And then, in 2005, as they are leaving a meeting with Iraqi partners, four CPT-ers are taken hostage by a group of extremists. Muslim friends in Iraq and throughout the Middle East condemn the action and ask for the peacemakers' release. International attention turns to the hostages. Off and on, they are in the news for months. "What were they doing there in the first place?" the news anchors ask. I watch friends try to reduce whole lives of conviction to sound bites.

One morning, after months of waiting, we get the news. Tom Fox, the lone American hostage, has been found dead on a garbage heap outside Baghdad, one bullet through his head and another through his heart. I think of his friends from the Quaker Meeting in Northern Virginia who came out to greet us just weeks before when we kept vigil with CPT outside the White House, praying for Tom and asking our country's president to listen to his witness.

Another way is possible, indeed. But it might cost you your life. People like Tom know this. Their lives have been claimed by a God who would rather die in love than guarantee justice by the threat of violence. Having found new life in Christ, Tom lived and died that love.

The witness of CPT, strange as it may seem, has a long precedent among God's people. When Moses declared to Pharaoh, "Let my people go!" he had no power to liberate the Hebrew children from slavery. But Moses had met the living God in a burning bush and was filled with holy boldness to declare that God could make a way out of no way. In a different context, when Babylon was the world power to deal with, three Israelites refused to bow down to a statue of the king and were thrown into a furnace of fire as punishment. As the book of Daniel remembers it, they came out of the fire without so much as a hint of smoke on their clothes. Someone said they'd seen a fourth person walking with them in the flames.

Stories like this remind God's people that the rulers and authorities of the world as we know it do not have the last word. Kings and presidents are used to people heeding their commands. If we do not, they have whole armies to encourage compliance. Violence is their trump card. But God's people remember that no king is higher than the King of the Universe and the Creator of life is stronger than death. If the law of the land contradicts the word of our Lord, we know whose command we must follow.

Jesus inhabits this tradition of divine obedience (and civil *dis*obedience) when he is called before King Herod and Pilate in Jerusalem. From his triumphal entry to his cleansing of the temple to his death as a political criminal, Jesus challenges worldly authority by submitting to his Father. "Not my will, but yours be done," he prays. Standing before earthly authorities, Jesus fulfills a long tradition of divine obedience over and against the powers that be in this world.

But Jesus is also doing a new thing.

Through his death and resurrection in the face of the powers that be, Jesus is inaugurating a new era in human history. If he really is the hope of Israel, then Jesus is not only the epitome of its best ideals, not just the incarnation of its deepest logic. Jesus is more than that. If Jesus is Messiah—if Israel's story advances to its conclusion in him—then something genuinely new has been actualized in Jesus' life, death, and resurrection. What the church finds "in Christ" is not one more goal to strive for, but a new way of being human.

Or, in the memorable summary of John's first epistle: "As he is, so are we in this world" (4:17, KJV).

In the early church, this conviction led Christians to expect a tension between their community and the governing authorities in the places where they lived. "A servant is not greater than his master," they recalled Jesus saying. "If they persecuted me, they will persecute you also" (John 15:20).

Though the new era of God's peaceable kingdom was real in the community of the Messiah, the early church knew from experience that the kingdoms of this world were also still present and very real. The advent of Messiah's reign had not immediately ended the kingdoms of this world, though their ultimate defeat was assured at the cross. Christians understood themselves to be living the way of the peaceable kingdom right alongside the violence of an order that was passing away. The challenge was not to overcome the world. Jesus had already done that. The challenge was to faithfully inhabit Jesus' way of engaging the powers.

The new thing they found in Jesus was a new way of being in the world.

When Christians gained considerable worldly power, first in the Roman Empire and subsequently in other kingdoms and nation states, Jesus' peculiar way of nonviolent love seemed less realistic and, to a growing number of believers, irresponsible. How can any authority both establish the rule of law and turn the other cheek? What decent person who had the power to stop a Hitler would not kill a tyrant to save a whole people? Still, as necessary as violence seemed to many Christians, the conviction that Jesus inaugurated a new era in human history has always meant that Christians have a problem with war. In order to name when war is unjust, and thus not permissible for any Christian, the church developed criteria for a "just war."

In considerations of the Christian tradition on war and peace, just war is often presented as the majority position over and against the minority stance of pacifism or Christian nonviolence. Such a presentation of church history, however, does not recognize the fact that just-war teaching always limited violence to adult men in police or military units. This actually excluded the vast majority of Christians from the use of violence, simply by virtue of their being women, children, clergy, monastics, or everyday citizens not engaged in a just war or police action. What is more, it was assumed for most of the church's history that participation in acts of violence — even acts deemed just — was a concession to the ways of the world that no doubt led Christians to sin. The church made provision for repentance and reconciliation — not celebration — when soldiers came home from battle. Even when war seems inevitable, our hope is not in military victory but in the reconciliation of all things through Jesus Christ.

When God's people hold onto the hope of reconciliation through the peculiar way of the cross, we interrupt the assumptions of a culture of violence. But the truth is that all of us—not just soldiers and police officers—are well practiced in the use of worldly power. Those of us who come from positions of privilege in society lean on the silent power of money and social norms, trusting in systems of control that have favored people who speak our language or share our skin color. At the same time, people who live with their backs against the wall resort to subversive acts of violence, carving out a space for survival by manipulating the fears of those who seem to be in control. We can see these dynamics at work in local and international political negotiations. And, if we pay attention, we can see the same habits worked out between husbands and wives, parents and children, bosses and coworkers, pastors and congregations.

In the world that is passing away, violence rules. But in the new world that has already begun, Jesus shows us a better way.

In the midst of a "war on terror," when soldiers are often celebrated as heroes in churches, it can be difficult for anyone —especially American Christians—to remember why we would rather die than kill. But to forget the peculiar witness of martyrs like Tom Fox is to forget the "new thing" that the New Testament celebrates as the unique sign of Christ's resurrection power. Because Christ is risen from the dead, a people exists that does not live by the power of violence. The church calls those who choose to die rather than kill "martyrs" because they show us the power of Christ's nonviolent love. We remember these saints as a way of reminding ourselves that no power deserves our allegiance more than the One who raised Jesus from the dead. No way is more trustworthy than the way of nonviolent love.

Communities of Peace

In the desert tradition there is a story about two monks who lived side by side for years without ever having any disagreement. "We should have an argument like other people," one brother said to the other. "I will take this brick and place it between us. I will say: 'It is mine,' and you can say: 'no, it's mine.' This is what leads to a dispute and a fight." Through years of prayer and life together, these brothers had learned about the source of human conflict. What is more, they knew they were not immune from it. So the one brother said to the other, "The brick is mine," and the other replied, "No, it's mine." They went back and forth like this until the second brother finally said, "Well, if it's yours, then take it."[10]

Monks who have lived together in community over generations remember this story because they know from experience how hard it is to give our lives over to the way of Jesus when we have to deal with other people. Those of us who have lived with spouses, siblings, or friends can empathize. We all have things we cling to—a favorite possession, our free time, a sense of control, the belief that we are right. When other people lay claim to these things, we feel threatened. Our gut reaction is to defend ourselves, and we use the power we have to do it. Maybe it's a harsh word or maybe it's a cold shoulder. Maybe it's the decision to leave. But even conflict avoidance can be an exercise in worldly power. When we trust our own power to overcome the differences between us, we are not trusting the way of Jesus.

The two monks in the desert cell knew this. Part of being a community of Christ's peace, they saw, was learning to fight fair and trust a power greater than the violence of an order that is passing away. They knew this because they read their Bible:

> If your brother or sister sins, go and point out their fault, just between the two of you. If they listen to you, you have won them over. But if they will not listen, take one or two others along, so that "every matter may be established by the testimony of two or three witnesses." If they still refuse to listen, tell it to the church; and if they refuse to listen even to the church, treat them as you would a pagan or a tax collector.
>
> Truly I tell you, whatever you bind on earth will be bound in heaven, and whatever you loose on earth will be loosed in heaven. (MATTHEW 18:15–18)

Maybe the most striking feature of this binding-and-loosing process that Jesus gives to the church is the initial instruction to point out other people's sins. To most of us this seems, at the very least, impolite. At its worst, it looks like the opposite of peace. (Especially if you've seen how this passage is often used to "discipline" brothers or sisters in some Christian communities.) How could picking a fight be the way to offer an alternative to this world's violence?

As a habit of our life together, truth-telling that leads to healthy conflict is the process Jesus offers for us to learn the way of peace. We are, as the ancient monks in their cell could see, like other people. We are broken and twisted by sin. To know the nonviolent love of Jesus isn't to escape from the patterns of this world's power, but to know that those patterns are interrupted through the patient practice of truth-telling and forgiveness. We learn to be a community of peace as we learn to see our sin through others' eyes and receive not only God's forgiveness, but theirs also. This process of disturbing the false peace of our relationships for the sake of receiving true peace is the way of Jesus. To follow him is to learn the peculiar practices of this way of living together.

Thinking about the petty differences we have with people close to us can seem like a completely difference subject than martyrdom in global conflicts, but the New Testament wants us to see how these two go together in a single way of life. Why Christians would rather die than kill is not only about why we have a problem with war, but also about why we persist in life together with people whom we often don't even like. "Whoever wants to be my disciple," Jesus said, "must deny themselves and take up their cross daily and follow me" (Luke 9:23). This cross that is necessary to discipleship is not the generalized suffering of humanity. As true as it may be that we all have burdens to bear, the particular burden of the cross is the cost of turning away from worldly power and trusting the power of Jesus' love, both in our most intimate relationships and in our political relationships.

In short, to live as communities of peace is to live in the conviction that we know in Christ a new way of engaging the world.

How we live in relationship to other people and the world around us is often called "ethics" in Christian teaching. Because all of us have to make decisions every day about what we are or are not going to do, ethics is often portrayed as decision making, especially in extreme situations. We often think ethics is about whether Christians should fight in war, have sex outside of marriage, practice in vitro fertilization, or "pull the plug" when a loved one is at the end of life. These are, indeed, ethical considerations. But if we are to make these kinds of decisions in Christ, it is more important for us to know the peculiar way of Christ in a community of peace than it is to think hard about what we would do in an extreme case.

In this regard, actual extreme cases sometimes make the point best. In the midst of World War II, when Nazi Germany was committed both to the extermination of Jewish people and to expansion in Europe, a village in occupied France quietly harbored hundreds of Jews, sparing their lives. Given the lack of resistance in so many places—and the high cost that so many resisters paid—it was a heroic act. Yet, when asked why they did it, most of the villagers simply said, "We never thought of not doing it." For years a priest named André Trocmé had patiently taught Jesus' example of forgiveness and nonviolent love at the village church. Over time, these people had become a community of peace. When the extreme case happened, the way of Jesus was an unquestioned habit.

"If anyone is in Christ," the apostle Paul wrote to the early church, "the new creation has come" (2 Corinthians 5:17). Yes, the patterns of an old and broken order continue, causing a great deal of suffering and frustration. But the advent of a whole new world is the basis of New Testament ethics. The "old nature" that Paul calls us to battle against is part of the old order that is passing away. It is the set of habits that humans developed in a world where violence had the last word. In Christ, however, we are raised to a new reality. Because this reality of new creation redefines how we see the world, it reframes our habits of social engagement.

In the ancient world, it was common practice to abandon unwanted children. For families who knew too well the limits of their resources, it was a hard but real fact that deformed or even female children were often more of a burden than a family could imagine bearing. Rather than watch the child suffer, the family would expose them to the elements after birth and end their suffering. Though circumstances are quite different today, the logic of these families is very similar to contemporary considerations around DNA testing and abortion. There is a realism that shapes most ethical considerations around family planning. Along with that realism, there is a certain understanding of what compassion looks like. Rather than watch an abnormal child suffer, doctors often advise ending their life in utero.

When the practice of child exposure was common, Christians were infamous for their "foolish" decision to take in children who were abandoned by their neighbors. Of course, these Christians faced the same harsh realities that their neighbors wrestled with in their decision whether to end a child's life. But the Christians also knew the reality of a community in which "the one who gathered much did not have too much, and the one who gathered little did not have too little" (2 Corinthians 8:15). No doubt, some of them suffered and even died for their decision. But like the people in the French village, they probably didn't think of it as a decision. Because their eyes were open to a new creation, they thought it better to die than to assume that the reality of death was a necessity.

The same is true for communities of peace today. Whether they choose to carry a baby with a genetic defect to term or to actively resist the violence of wars, disciples take up their cross and follow Jesus not because they have learned to make the hard choice in an extreme case, but because they can't imagine acting differently in light of the good news they have heard and seen. Their habit of choosing life is one they have learned by getting to know the way of Jesus among the people who are Christ's body. It is, for the most part, slow and undramatic work. It is also how God chooses to engage our world in love.

Resurrection Power

Every tradition of ethical consideration is based on some fundamental conviction which, over time, has shaped a community's conversation about how best to live in the world. If you pay close attention to American law and the conversation it sums up, a fundamental conviction about the freedom of individuals emerges. This is a country that was founded by people who did not want to be told what to do. If, on the other hand, we pay attention to the ethical considerations of Native Americans, a different core conviction is manifest: every decision is to be made in light of how it will affect future generations. Here is a people who learned over time that humans cannot survive if each of us only thinks about ourselves.

If the ethical conversations of a community reveal its core conviction, what does Christian ethics reveal about what we really believe?

This is an important question for the church to ask because it forces us to think about how our actions often betray a lack of trust in the way of Jesus. When we reason, for example, that the generosity of Jesus' command to "give to everyone who asks" (Luke 6:30) must be checked by the responsibility to "take care of our own" or to not enable the "undeserving poor," we acknowledge that we have a notion of responsibility that is more important to us than obedience to our Lord's command. Or when we say that we must be realistic in our expectations about creation care, acknowledging that so much of the way we live is dependent on an unsustainable use of the earth's resources, we confess a fundamental conviction that the reality of the world as we know it is simply the way things have to be.

All of this is sadly true of the community that gathers in Jesus' name. If there is a line that separates the way of the world from the way of Christ, it runs through each of us. Still, the language of Christian ethics helps us to name the core conviction of those who have found new life in Christ. Whenever we say no to the necessity of this world's power in scorn of the consequences—whenever we say as a community that we would rather die than kill—we confess that Christ is risen from the dead. The core conviction undergirding Christian ethics is the power of the resurrection.

Tom Fox gave his life in nonviolent love not because he thought that such a sacrifice would convert his killers or bring an end to the war in Iraq. He knew it was better to die than kill because he knew the power of God to raise Jesus from the dead. If God has shown us a better way, we can trust it whatever the consequences. Even if obedience leads us to our death—even if it means that others may have to suffer—we serve the God who is able to breathe new life onto dry bones and who "calls into being things that were not" (Romans 4:17). If our God raised Jesus from the dead, then no power on earth can demand our allegiance.

This is as true in considerations of individual morality as it is in questions of war and peace. Consider, for example, how our fundamental convictions are manifest in a typical conversation with teenagers about premarital sex. In an attempt to persuade young people, often against their bodies' desire and their friends' practice, that sex is made for marriage, Christians employ a wide range of tactics. On the one hand, Christian adults often try to explain how much better sex is if young people wait for marriage. Faithfulness, then, becomes an issue of delayed gratification—"true love waits," we say, and then we try to find people who can testify to the goodness of patience. But because there will always be someone who can testify to the joys of premarital sex, Christians often swing to the opposite extreme and highlight the dangers of premarital sex. Broken hearts. STDs. Unwanted pregnancies. Testimonies abound here also. Still, many teenagers are unconvinced.

Of course, everyone knows what the church is saying to do—or *not* to do, in this case. But they may also notice the fundamental conviction behind these ways of reasoning. The point of sex, it seems, is to have the best experience with the least amount of danger. The main point of one of life's most important activities, it seems, is to have fun and be safe. Whatever Christian teenagers end up doing, is this really the conviction that the church wants to communicate to them?

If the power of the resurrection is real, then we can trust it to compel teenagers with a greater force than biology, self-discipline, or fear. "The body ... is not meant for sexual immorality, but for the Lord," Paul wrote to the early church at Corinth (1 Corinthians 6:13). If we are in Christ, we have more important things to do with our body than simply making them feel good or keeping them safe. Our bodies have been claimed for full time service to God. Bored teenagers need nothing so much as a challenge to give their lives to something bigger than themselves. But this is not just "something." Paul is inviting all of us to give ourselves to God's movement to redeem the whole universe. "By his power God raised the Lord from the dead, and he will raise us also" (6:14). This is why the New Testament says we don't sleep with our girlfriends.

It's also why we don't lie, why we speak kindly to one another, why we scorn greed and bitterness, anger and fear. "You must no longer live as the Gentiles do," Paul writes, "in the futility of their thinking. They are darkened in their understanding and separated from the life of God.... You were taught, with regard to your former way of life, to put off your old self, which is being corrupted by its deceitful desires; to be made new in the attitude of your minds; and to put on the new self, created to be like God in true righteousness and holiness" (Ephesians 4:17–18, 22–24). Because Christ is risen from the dead, we are a people who would rather die to ourselves than to continue in the habits that lead everyone toward death. Because the way of the world is as present in war making as it is in sexual immorality, every single act of faithfulness is charged with cosmic significance. We remember the saints as our heroes and heroines because they trusted the way of Jesus even to the point of death. Imitating them, we imitate Christ, echoing the old gospel hymn:

> Must Jesus bear his cross alone
> and all the world go free?
> No, there's a cross for everyone,
> and there's a cross for me.[11]

In seventeenth-century France, Nicholas Herman was an ambitious young man who fought in the Thirty Years War and worked in the household of a prominent French banker. He understood the ways of the world, and he showed some promise of climbing from his relatively humble social position to greater heights in French society. But after a powerful conversion experience in early adulthood, Nicholas grew more and more suspicious of the ways of the world. An uncle who was a monk told him, "The air of the world is so contagious that if it does not strike dead all who breathe it, it inevitably alters or corrupts the morals of those who follow its ways."

Determined to embrace the way of Jesus, Nicholas quit his job and devoted himself to prayer. But he soon found that he was not very good at silent prayer because his mind wandered and he lost focus easily. Hoping to learn from others, he joined a monastery, taking the name Brother Lawrence. Sadly, Lawrence found that he didn't get much better at prayer. Even when saying the liturgy with others, he was easily distracted. Left to his own, he was hopeless. Yet in the midst of his struggle, Brother Lawrence discovered that when doing the simple tasks he was assigned to — sweeping the floor or washing pots in the kitchen — he could talk with God. Though he was the "worst" of God's servants, he could enjoy fellowship with the Lord of the universe while giving himself away in service. He called this "practicing the presence of God."[12]

The fact that Christians would rather die than kill does not mean that dramatic acts of martyrdom are the hallmark of our faith. We remember Tom Fox and the power of Christ's resurrection that is manifest in his witness. But we also remember Brother Lawrence. Though he died in obscurity, his commitment to "die daily" in simple service is a testament to the radical new way of life that the power of resurrection makes possible in the world. "You know that the rulers of the Gentiles lord it over them," Jesus said to his disciples on the way to the cross. "Not so with you. Instead, whoever wants to become great among you must be your servant, and whoever wants to be first must be your slave — just as the Son of Man did not come to be served, but to serve, and to give his life as a ransom for many" (Matthew 20:25–28).

The struggle for worldly power is like a game of King of the Hill: only one person can be at the top—and never for very long. But Jesus shows us a better way. If greatness means service, then anyone can be great. If we would rather die than kill, then God can raise us up to live the kind of life that lasts forever.

CHAPTER 8

Why We Share Good News

I AM SITTING ACROSS THE DINNER TABLE FROM EMILY AND Pedro, wondering how much of their story they want to share amidst the interruptions of dishes passing, water glasses getting filled, and children asking how much they have to eat before they can get up and go play. I decide to open the door and let them decide how far to invite us in. "So, how have ya'll been doing?" A minute later, all twenty-five people in the room are listening to a story about how this family's whole life changed.

I know before I ask that Pedro spent the past nineteen months in Stuart Detention Center, a regional holding center for US Immigration and Customs Enforcement. "I'm just soaking it in," Pedro says, smiling. "It feels so good to be free." But the relief is mixed with simple exhaustion for this family that has been stretched across three states for the better part of two years, wondering if they would ever be together again because of a court order that went to the wrong mailing address. For Pedro it has been a crash course in surviving a system of mass incarceration. "We had no support in there," he says. "We had to learn to take care of each other."

Emily too has been on a steep learning curve. After realizing that the system offers no support to family members either, she set out to find the help she needed while holding down a fulltime job and taking care of two-year-old Logan. She knew she couldn't do this alone. A strange mix of lawyers and activists, hospitality houses and outdoor vigils emerged on the landscape of rural Georgia, around this place that had swallowed up her husband and would not let him go. Emily watched her mother get arrested in an act of civil disobedience, alongside people who'd never met Pedro. She held onto hope as thousands of people signed a petition asking for his release. In the end, the decision was a federal judge's to make. He ruled in their favor, and Pedro came home. But they know it could have gone the other way. Pedro can't forget the three thousand people he left behind when he walked out of the prison gates.

"How do you keep from being angry?" a young man leans forward to ask. "I'm angry just hearing your story." Pedro and Emily are quiet for a moment. "Well, for one thing," Emily starts, "I didn't know God before all this happened." We have been listening to a conversion story, I realize, and I look again at the couple sitting across from me. Here are two apostles who have been born again, testifying to what they have seen and heard in God's movement to interrupt our broken world with a new creation. Telling their story, they are sharing the truth that has put on flesh in rural Georgia. But they are more than storytellers. They are evangelists proclaiming the good news that has changed their life.

From the earliest days of the Christian movement, people

who encountered Jesus in the flesh became heralds of God's message, crafting words with tongue and pen to say how the whole world had changed before their eyes. In the gospels, when Jesus was still making his way to Jerusalem, he invested a great deal of energy in asking people *not* to talk about the interruptive power of God they were witnessing. Such news, Jesus was clear, can spread *too* fast. Nevertheless, he was equally clear that a time for testimony would come: "When you are brought before synagogues, rulers and authorities, do not worry about how you will defend yourselves or what you will say, for the Holy Spirit will teach you at that time what you should say" (Luke 12:11–12). Jesus said that those who followed his way after him would be his "witnesses," testifying before friends, strangers, and even ruling authorities that the whole world had changed. This is "news" in its truest sense—a notification that something out of the ordinary has happened that is of genuine public interest. More important than the election of a president or a declaration of war, the gospel of Jesus announces a transformation that, if it is true, changes everything. This is front page material.

So it was that Peter stood before the temple authorities in Jerusalem and declared about the Jesus they had recently sentenced to death: "Salvation is found in no one else, for there is no other name under heaven given to people by which we must be saved" (Acts 4:12). Such boldness was inspired by the fact that Jesus had not stayed dead, but rose again on the third day, demonstrating the power of God. This resurrection power was not only confirmed by the empty tomb (which could be, and was, explained in other ways), but also by the transformed lives of those who had been with Jesus. In short, ethics and evangelism went together in the early church. The evidence of the gospel's truth was a community of people who lived by the logic of death and resurrection.

Understanding ourselves as Christ's body, the bearers of God's mission in the world, the church has always been committed to evangelism — the proclamation of God's good news to every people and place, system and authority. When Christianity was a minority movement, this message often sounded like a lost cause to those who held power. Early Christianity's strength was not in its watertight arguments or mass appeal, but in the distinct witness of those who shouted its truth with their whole lives. But in those places where Christians became a cultural majority, the articulation of gospel truth got mixed up with self-justifying narratives and worldly power. Evangelism, in this context, was often divorced from the way of Jesus, leading to forced conversions, Crusades that killed in the name of Christ, and imperialism that mixed universal truth claims with culturally conditioned norms and biases. A great deal of evil has been done in the name of spreading good news.

Both Christians and non-Christians in the West today live with this memory of the church's mixed history. On the one hand, many public institutions with Christian origins clearly contribute toward the common good. A secular agnostic in America doesn't blink an eye when writing a check to support the Red *Cross* or donating an old couch to the *Salvation* Army. Still, this citizen of post-Christendom society usually distrusts the institutional church, is put off by the seemingly exclusive claims of Christian doctrine, and sees faith as something we should move beyond in pursuit of higher ideals, like justice and reason.

Painfully aware of our shortcomings, Christians often don't know how to talk to someone like this about Jesus. We are tempted to reduce Jesus to a personal savior so we can engage others in the public square on their own terms. When we succumb to this temptation, evangelism is reduced to either the saving of souls or the doing of good deeds. Conservative Christians maintain the truth claim of the gospel while limiting its scope. The gospel message, though it is for everyone, is no longer front-page material. It fits better in a "Faith and Life" section, touching the hearts of the faithful and inspiring them to share their religious experience with others. More liberal Christians point out that this approach to evangelism ignores the social implications of the gospel message. But while they recognize the broad scope of the good news, they hesitate to identify themselves with a truth that seems to exclude others' traditions. The good news has front-page implications, but biblical language seems far too exclusive in a pluralistic society. So evangelism, for the liberal, becomes digging wells and building orphanages. Who could be against that, after all?

Well, it depends on the story that tells us who we are. If we believe, as the social Darwinists have, that the salvation of humanity is wrapped up in a natural selection of superior races, we have good reason *not* to dig wells and build orphanages for some people. Such compassion slows the end of history for which our whole story teaches us to hope. But even if we trust a story that assumes helping people to survive is a good, we still have to figure out how we are going to live after we've survived childhood or our basic need for water has been met. While orphanages and wells might be goods common to several stories, *why* they are goods has everything to do with the end our story points us toward.

Christians share good news—we tell the story in which Jesus Christ is the hope of the world—because we believe that the *why* behind our actions has everything to do with the substance of our hope. In short, hope has its reasons because hope is more than a feeling that all people hold in common though they name it different ways. Hope that is real is rooted in truth. This truth is not some power that Christians possess and wield like a nuclear weapon; it is, rather, a person who has revealed himself to us in love. Because God's love is freely given, we share it freely, knowing that it has the power to overcome our world's deepest darkness.

Emily and Pedro are evangelists because their life was saved by the gospel's hope. According to another story, they might be seen as either a threat to homeland security or a victory for the peace and justice community. But neither of these are the stories that best narrate their experience. They know hope because when it looked like all was lost they met a group of people who were willing to lay down their lives in self-giving love. That is, they met a body that was Christ to them.

"I didn't know God before all this happened," Emily says to us around the table. Because she met Jesus outside a detention center in Georgia, we see hope face-to-face at dinner.

Learning to Tell the Truth

At a minimum security women's prison in North Carolina, Sarah teaches a class each fall on spiritual autobiography. Half of the women in this class come from outside the prison walls. They are enrolled in graduate programs at local universities, honing their skills in a particular discipline (almost always one that includes storytelling). The other half of the class wears state-issued green clothes and walks from the dorm building across the prison yard. Together these women read memoirs from Christians, Muslims, and agnostics alike. They wrestle with the lives of public figures like Dorothy Day and Malcolm X alongside little-known memoirists who've chronicled their search for truth in the everyday circumstances of raising kids and keeping house. Alongside their reading, these women take on a semester-long project of telling their own stories.

A writing class, this seminar behind bars is an exercise in both paying attention to how others tell their stories and learning to tell your own. Early in the class, Sarah always does an exercise to help the students learn to name types of stories —the hero tale, the victim's saga, the damsel in distress, the seeker on a quest. While the students see quickly how the movies they've watched and the books they've read fit these types, it's always something of a surprise for them to see how their own story is shaped by stories that have been told time and again.

For the students, this realization presents a difficult question: If my life is shaped by a story bigger than me and my decisions, how do I know whether that story is true? It takes more than a semester to get to the bottom of a question like that. But a writing class can be a good place to start.

Christians have told and retold the story of Jesus for two millennia not only because we believe it is true, but also because it's a story that helps us tell the truth about ourselves. The women in Sarah's class discover through writing something that all of us have to deal with eventually: we have no place to stand outside our own stories to judge what is true and what is not. While we might name different types of stories and make choices about how we're going to interpret our experiences and decisions, we always do this as people who've already been shaped by a story we inherited. No one gets to start from scratch. But each of us, from within the story we've received, decides whether we will continue to trust what we first received or inhabit a different story. This decision is what we usually call "faith."

The Bible says that faith is the "substance of things hoped for, the evidence of things not seen" (Hebrews 11:1, KJV). Faith is what we trust for those questions that we cannot know the answer to, for the presuppositions that undergird whatever story we call our own. In the modern world we are in the habit of thinking that faith matters for our personal and religious lives. When we talk about "people of faith," we usually refer to people who are committed Muslims or Buddhists, Jews or Christians. On the other hand, we usually assume that what matters in economics and politics, science and medicine is facts, not faith. Religion is about what we believe while science is about what we know.

But good scientists agree with the women in Sarah's writing seminar that whatever we know (including the facts), we know within a story that we have chosen to trust. That is, we are all people of faith. Of course, doubt plays a role in the pursuit of truth for scientists, just as it does for theologians. But none of us can ever doubt everything. Whether the truth we seek is best described as scientific or religious, our pursuit of it depends on holding experience up against the story we assume to be true. In science, when the facts demand a new story to explain how they can all be true, we call that necessary change a "paradigm shift." When the facts of our lives cry out for a story that can help us tell the truth about ourselves, we call it "conversion."

For Jesus, the invitation to welcome God's story is a call to conversion: "The kingdom of God has come near. Repent and believe the good news" (Mark 1:15). To trust that what Jesus says about the world is true is to, quite literally, have a change of mind. This conversion—this paradigm shift—does not invalidate the truth of the story that came before it. In calling God's people to conversion, Jesus says, "Do not think I have come to abolish the law or the prophets; I have not come to abolish them but to fulfill them." The new story that Jesus brings incorporates the truth of the old, offering both a framework for understanding what we knew before and a lens for seeing truth we could not recognize within our old story. Even so, the only way people who have inhabited one story can learn to trust another is to experience a change of mind. We must be "born again," as Jesus says to Nicodemus in John's gospel (3:3). Or, more literally, we must be "reconceived from above." That is to say, conversion is about reimagining our human story from the place where Jesus starts his—not with the mixing of two human stories, but with the miraculous union of God's story and a human story. Christian teaching about the virgin birth tells us that Jesus' unique life was conceived when the Holy Spirit impregnated a woman named Mary. We can't explain how that happened any more than we can explain the physics that preceded the Big Bang. But the virgin birth is the story Christians trust to explain why each of us must be reconceived from above.

By trusting this story, we learn something about how the gospel both affirms and challenges every human story. Because Jesus is born of the union between God's story and a particular human story, we know that the truth of the particular stories we inhabit is not denied. Whatever truth there is in Islam or Romanticism, in capitalism or Buddhism, that truth is God's truth. Within the overarching story of Creation and Fall, this is truth that has not been clouded by sin from people who were created in God's image. And yet, because every human story has found its shape in the context of sin, each of us needs to be interrupted by grace to see how the truth we can see points us toward the truth we cannot see. Jesus says we must be "reconceived from above," so that God can rewrite our personal and cultural stories with a miraculous infusion of God's very self.

We share good news, then, neither to show our neighbors why Christianity is "right" nor to save people from the corrupting influence of other religions, but to name the story that helps us tell the truth about ourselves.

At a women's college in Massachusetts, I'm on campus to

talk to a Christian undergraduate fellowship about peace-making in the Middle East. Because it's Friday, the Muslim women's group is gathering at noon for their weekly prayers. Someone from their group hears about my visit and invites me to join them. Would I share something about my experiences in Iraq? Trying to say why I chose to disobey State Department orders and stay in Baghdad as it was being bombed, I share about wrestling with the powers of consumerism and nationalism in my life. "I started to see that it's hard to be a Christian in America," I say. Immediately, I see a look of recognition.

"It's hard to be a Muslim in America too," one young woman says. And I spend the rest of the hour listening to Muslim women share about the temptations of wealth and technology, greed and self-indulgence. We only have an hour and so don't have much time to talk about the differences between Christianity and Islam. But I walk away thankful for something that Christianity and Islam share in common. These women are living a story that offers them considerable resources for telling the truth about who they are in a world subject to the powers of sin and death.

That Our Healing May Be Complete

Christianity does not offer a program to fix the world. It claims, instead, that the world has been redeemed in the life, death, and resurrection of Jesus Christ. We trust this good news because it is our one true hope. And we keep telling the story because we know that none of us have trusted it completely. Yes, we have been saved in Christ. But our healing is not complete until the truth of the gospel's story works itself down into the darkest reaches of our hearts and our world, healing those things that are broken and restoring the parts of God's good creation that have been crushed. As people who know the story of Jesus, we share good news so that we can be healed through the reconciling work God makes possible in Christ.

I met Alvin when he was fifteen years old, wandering the streets of our neighborhood and glad to talk to anyone who had time to listen. I hadn't known him long when he told me that his father killed his mother when Alvin was five years old. "If there is a God, I don't like him," Alvin said.

One evening, when he was sixteen, Alvin came by our house after his evening shift with a catering company. He often stopped in to share leftovers and talk. This particular evening, he had a terrible pain in his side. We carried him to the emergency room, and they performed an appendectomy. When the hospital discharged him, he came home with us to recover.

To a teenager who was used to fending for himself, a home felt like good news. We invited Alvin to stay. Given his experience, though, Alvin was cautious about the fact that we gathered to pray first thing every morning and again at night. "Do I have to come?" he asked. "No," we said. "We pray because we want to spend time with God. No one has to come." For the next two years, he avoided those prayer times like the plague.

When Alvin graduated from high school, we were there

to cheer him on, along with other friends from our community and his extended family. We did what we could to help him go to college, and he chose a historically black university with a required freshman course in the African-American experience. The week his class read Martin Luther King, Alvin called home to say, "I think I'm starting to understand what ya'll are about." Our community continued to walk with Alvin, navigating the unexpected twists and turns of life. After we helped him through a particularly difficult (and expensive) bout with dental trouble, Alvin said to me, "I still don't like God, but I'm starting to like Christians."

All of this time, I prayed for Alvin. I prayed that he would know the love of God in the friendship of people who loved him no matter what he said or did. I prayed that he would learn to trust the good news of Jesus by seeing it put into practice. I prayed these prayers, but I didn't realize what it would cost.

One night, when Alvin was still a teenager, I was sitting across from him at the table in our kitchen, arguing about a window he had broken to get into the house after he lost his key for the fourth time. All the things I hadn't said over the years added intensity to the words I was saying, and Alvin decided he'd had enough. He got up and walked out. Not thinking at the moment what it would look like to the neighbors, I chased him into the street. One block down, at the intersection with Knox Street, he turned back to look at me, and there were tears in his eyes. My vision blurred as cool streams started pouring across my own hot cheeks. Both of us stood there, helpless. Finally, we turned in silence and walked home together.

That moment at the corner of Knox and Berkeley Streets, as I stood embarrassed before Alvin and my neighbors, was an experience of conversion for me. The story I knew about how God's healing love is made real in a community that shares good news with our whole lives was interrupted by my own deep need to be healed and forgiven and made new in Christ. This young man I had prayed for was showing me the healing that I needed. Somehow, the open wound of his deep pain had touched a pain in me that only God could heal. My prayer for him, I suddenly realized, was a prayer for myself. If either of us was going to be healed, we would be healed together.

In the New Testament, that word *healed* is the same as the word "saved." Jesus heals the sick, makes the lame to walk and the blind to see as a way of proclaiming that God's salvation is here. Holistic healing that saves us from the power of death is the heart of God's mission in the world. This healing is as concrete as a home for the homeless, a meal for the hungry, a cup of cold water for someone who is thirsty. If salvation does not touch the material conditions of our lives, it is no salvation at all.

But salvation is also the forgiveness of sins and the healing of hearts. Salvation reaches into the depths of our being and remakes us.

In Luke's gospel, when a man who cannot walk is brought to Jesus by some friends, Jesus says to the man, "Your sins are forgiven." These four words immediately stir up the local religious leaders who made it their business to name and forgive sins. In response to their anxiety, Jesus asks, "Which is easier: to say, 'Your sins are forgiven,' or to say, 'Get up and walk'?" (Matthew 9:2, 5). The answer is clear. A doctor might be able to heal your body, but only God can forgive sins. Salvation is never smaller than the restoration of all creation to the peace and justice for which the world was made. But all healing, at its core, depends on the power of forgiveness.

People who are frustrated by a church that makes truth claims without embodying hope often quote a line attributed to Saint Francis: "Preach the gospel at all times; when necessary, use words." But Francis, who started an order of mendicant preachers, knew well that the good news we proclaim with our lives depends on all of us getting the truth of these words deep down into our bones: "Your sins are forgiven."

In the bag that I carry with me everywhere I preach, I keep a note that Alvin wrote me years ago, after we'd had it out on the street corner in our neighborhood.

> I wish I could take back all of those selfish things I have done in the past, along with all the harm I have done to our relationship. But I can't take these things back. All I can do is try to make amends and apologize. Although I'm terrible at all of this, I'm trying to the max. I'm sorry.

The good news of Jesus is that before our "I'm sorry," while we were still yelling at one another, angry on the street corner, God died for us. Before our "I'm sorry," Jesus says, "Your sins are forgiven."

We share good news because we know that nothing is more important in all the world than to know that we've been loved by the God who made us, by the God who wants us, by the God who won't give up on us no matter what we do. Maybe saying that with everything you are to someone else is the only way any of us ever know what it means to say it's true. To know the healing that God's love brings is to know that no pain that separates us from another person—no wound that alienates us from creation—is so great that it has not been overwhelmed by God's love.

To know this healing is to want to share it with everyone you meet.

Epilogue

AMERICA HAS A TRADITION OF GREAT AWAKENINGS — TIMES when we remember the Spirit blowing across our land and demonstrating God's power in people's lives. These revivals have renewed the church in our culture, giving rise to new denominations and swelling the ranks of the faithful. They've also pricked the conscience of this nation's soul, sparking reform movements from the abolitionists of the nineteenth century to the "What Would Jesus Do?" campaign of the early twentieth century. Our history teaches us to hope for a Great Awakening.

We have good reason for this hope. The God whom we know in Jesus has not abandoned us.

But the awakening that happens when the Spirit blows across our lives does not have to be "great" — at least, not if *great* means crowds of people filing into open fields or stadiums to hear talented communicators articulate the good news for our day. When Peter, "filled with the Holy Spirit," testified to God's power in the early days of the Christian movement, he wasn't noticed because of his communication savvy. People listened to Peter because they saw signs of hope in the new community he and John were part of. What they noted was that he and his friends had "been with Jesus." They had been given power to lead a different kind of life (see Acts 4:13).

So maybe we're not waiting for the next Great Awakening. Maybe we don't need another George Whitfield or Charles Finney, a Dwight Moody or Billy Graham. Maybe the Spirit is already breathing new life into the church and into God's good world through the everyday awakenings that are happening all around.

In hundreds—maybe thousands—of little communities that are mostly overlooked, people are being stirred by the Spirit to lead a different kind of life. It's a life that doesn't make sense if the gospel isn't true. But because these people have been with Jesus—because they've somehow gotten the truth of God's story deep down in their bones—their life does make sense.

Indeed, the way of Jesus is now the only way of living that makes any sense at all.

To see your life from this vantage point is to see a whole new world of possibility. It's like waking up from a bad dream to realize the thing that most scared you—the thing that just a moment before was as real as the price of gas—was only an illusion.

The way things are is not the way things have to be.

There is a new creation all around us.

It's an everyday awakening that can happen anywhere. When it does, you know you've found what you were looking for. You don't have to go somewhere else to find the answer. Your desperate search is over because God has met you where you are.

THE **AWAKENING** OF
HOPE

Book and DVD

How to Use
This Discussion Guide

The Awakening of Hope: Why We Practice a Common Faith is grounded in a deep conviction that God is stirring something new in our lives and in our world. From the very beginning of this project, Shane Claiborne and I dreamed of not only telling stories about the signs of hope we see in our world today, but also introducing you to some of the living saints who've passed their faith down to us. We're so excited to share the six-session *The Awakening of Hope* DVD that introduces you to some of the folks who've helped us catch the gospel bug.

This discussion guide was developed as a resource for groups to reengage Christian faith and share it with others in the way that living things spread best—through breath and touch, conversation and conversion. It guides a group through the basic questions of this book, connecting both with the lives of friends we introduce in the DVD and with teachings about the core convictions of our faith.

As I wrote in chapter 1, our efforts to live faithfully always include action and reflection. The pictures of hope that grab our attention point us toward God and the Big Questions.

This guide is designed to facilitate conversation about God and the Big Questions.

We hope you'll make a meal, invite your friends over, and let this guide lead you into conversations about the things that stir your soul.

For those who are both reading the book and watching the DVD, it might be helpful to know how the six sessions of the DVD match up with the chapters of the book:

DVD Session	Book Chapter(s)
1. Why We Eat Together	Chapters 2 & 3
2. Why We Make Promises	Chapter 4
3. Why It Matters Where We Live	Chapter 5
4. Why We Live Together	Chapter 6
5. Why We Would Rather Die Than Kill	Chapter 7
6. Why We Share Good News	Chapter 8

Format

The following format offers an outline for each of the six planned sessions. But there is enough material for groups who are using the book to split each session and stretch the study over twelve meetings. Feel free to use these pieces in whatever way makes the most sense for your group.

Living the Question

These opening questions serve to start the conversation by considering ways the "why" question for each session connects with participants' everyday lives.

DVD Viewing

The DVD length for each session is approximately 15–20 minutes long.

Listening to Lived Theology

These questions invite the group to consider the content of the DVD session and discuss the core conviction that each story highlights.

Listening to Scripture and Tradition

These questions focus on a Bible passage or core Christian teaching that helps the group go deeper in their consideration of faith.

Living the Life

These questions and ideas invite groups to consider how they can embody and practice the convictions they have considered in each session.

JONATHAN WILSON-HARTGROVE

Why We Eat Together

Living the Question

Everyone eats most every day—most of us more than once. Often the question on our mind is "What do I feel like eating?" or "Which sandwich is the cheapest?" But if we stop to think about it, eating also raises questions about where food comes from, what it connects us to, who we eat with, and why it matters.

1. Think about how, when, and where you eat. What basic questions about life does this daily activity raise for you?

2. Some people grew up saying grace with their families before meals. Did you? What's your reaction when you see someone bow to pray before a meal at a restaurant? Why do you think people of faith have often connected prayer and worship with eating?

DVD Viewing

Watch the "Why We Eat Together" session from the DVD.

Listening to Lived Theology

1. Shane begins by talking about how the cross is a symbol for three dimensions of reconciliation. While the vertical and horizontal dimensions are often the focus of contemporary Christian preaching, a reconciliation that is "anchored and rooted in the earth" is often not. How does it change your understanding of Christianity to think about the cross having an "earthy" dimension?

2. Chris Haw talks about the "Scriptural sin of slavery" that he sees in a place like Camden, where people suffer because someone else does not want to make their living by the sweat of their own brow. How does this way of talking about "sin" help you name the problems you see in the world? What is the connection between "sin" and broken social systems?

> *Chickens are part of salvation because they're part of creation.... All things are in the created order and they deserve respect and affection and appreciation for what they are. Salvation is for the whole planet, so affection and caretaking for all parts of the planet are part of the deal.*
> —CHRIS HAW

Shane talks about God's story in Scripture as being "not about escaping this world, but about bringing heaven to earth. It's about a resurrection story—that life conquers death, that grass can pierce concrete, that creation can be restored." How can this hope be reflected in the way we eat together? How might it be stifled by the ways we eat?

Come, Holy Spirit, and heal all that is broken in our lives, in our streets, and in our world.

Listening to Scripture and Tradition

Read this account of creation from the book of Genesis. Pay attention to the importance of ground and soil, food and eating in this story.

Genesis 2:4–9; 15–17

This is the account of the heavens and the earth when they were created, when the LORD God made the earth and the heavens.

Now no shrub had yet appeared on the earth and no plant had yet sprung up, for the LORD God had not sent rain on the earth and there was no one to work the ground, but streams came up from the earth and watered the whole surface of the ground. Then the LORD God formed a man from the dust of the ground and breathed into his nostrils the breath of life, and the man became a living being.

Now the LORD God had planted a garden in the east, in Eden; and there he put the man he had formed. The LORD God made all kinds of trees grow out of the ground—trees that were pleasing to the eye and good for food. In the middle of the garden were the tree of life and the tree of the knowledge of good and evil....

The LORD God took the man and put him in the

Garden of Eden to work it and take care of it. And the LORD God commanded the man, "You are free to eat from any tree in the garden; but you must not eat from the tree of the knowledge of good and evil, for when you eat from it you will certainly die."

1. How is our basic need for food reflected in this story? If this is the story that tells you what it means to be human, what connections can you make between soil, food, and your life?

2. What other stories try to tell us what it means to be human? What role do dirt and food play in those stories?

3. Why does the LORD instruct the human not to eat from the tree of the knowledge of good and evil? What does it mean that our most basic temptation as humans is a temptation to eat what we've been told not to?

Food isn't only at the beginning of our human story. It's also at the heart of the story we learn to live in Jesus Christ. In chapter 2, Jonathan:

It's no accident that the Lord's Supper—or Eucharist—has been the centerpiece of Christian worship from the church's earliest days. To remind us of what God's love looks like in the world, Jesus gave us a meal—bread to be his body and wine as his life-blood, poured out for friends and enemies alike. Throughout the past two thousand years of church history, this meal has scandalized the status quo, bringing Jews and Gentiles, slaves and slave-owners, citizens and undocumented neighbors together at the same table. This revolutionary meal inspired black and white people across the American South to sit down at segregated lunch counters in 1960, insisting that they should be served together because they were equal in the eyes of the Lord. The white citizens who spat in their faces and put cigarettes out on their heads knew that it's no small thing for people to eat together.

4. Why is the Lord's Supper a scandal? What does it interrupt? And how does that interruption help us name what's wrong in our world?

5. At the heart of the Christian faith is the conviction that Jesus, who is God-in-flesh, willingly died to address the first humans' choice to eat from the forbidden tree. The Lord's Supper is a "memorial" meal, meant to remind us of this loving sacrifice. How does the way Christians eat reflect convictions about who Jesus is and why he died?

Living the Life

1. Does seeing yourself as a creature change the way you think about eating? How?

2. How does the Lord's Supper invite you to think differently about your daily dinner? Or your family's Thanksgiving meal?

Ideas for putting faith into practice ...

- Plan a really nice dinner party at your home—the kind you'd plan if a friend were getting married—and invite folks from your local homeless shelter or group home to come be your guests.

- Pick one dish from the dinner you ate tonight and see if you can trace it all the way back to its source. Where did it grow? Who cared for it? Whose sacrifices made this food possible?

- Fast for a day with other members of your group. Collect the money that you would have spent on food and drinks and send it to an organization that's working to end hunger.

Why We Make Promises

Living the Question

Our lives are filled with people, projects, and causes that demand our attention, yet many of us are hesitant to ask for or make definitive commitments. We worry about people who seem too sure of their promises. Even when we think something is important, we often ask others to commit to it by making a case for how *little* they'll have to do. By most estimates, we live in a low-commitment culture.

1. Think about the people and organizations that have asked for your commitment. Who have you committed yourself to? Is there a public sign of that commitment? What do you and others need to keep that commitment?

2. What sort of commitments scare you? Share a story about why it can be hard to trust others' promises or make them yourself.

DVD Viewing

Watch the "Why We Make Promises" session from the DVD.

Listening to Lived Theology

The wisdom of Jean's life is a wisdom of knowing that because God has loved us and because God has called us and because God has been faithful to us, it is possible for us to be faithful to one another over the long haul, to have real community and be committed to one another in a covenant.
—JONATHAN WILSON-HARTGROVE

1. Jean Vanier talks about drawing strength from the permanence of his commitment to people with disabilities at L'Arche. How does making a permanent commitment to someone change your relationship with that person?

2. Jean says, "It's a long road to growth, and it begins just by living together." How do we pace ourselves if we're on a "long road" together? What kind of support might you need to learn the patience Jean is suggesting?

The beginning was essentially to do good in the name of Jesus. But the strength I had was I knew it was an irreversible act, that you don't do that with someone and then say, "Bye-bye!" So that gave me the space to change, to have fun.... The strength I had was that I knew this was what Jesus wanted. And then there was the gradual discovery that I was being healed by these people. It was just good to live together. —JEAN VANIER

3. Jean speaks emphatically about the "unity of our humanity," and says, "People with disabilities have gifts to give the church—gifts of simplicity, of laughter, of fun." How does commitment make a different kind of "fun" possible? What do we learn from Jesus about who we should commit ourselves to? And how?

Listening to Scripture and Tradition

In chapter 4, Jonathan wrote, "We make promises because they mark us as people who are turning from the rebellion of original sin to life with God in the membership of a new creation. Making promises reminds us that our lives have been claimed by God's promise. The biblical name for this is 'covenant.'"

Read the following passage together:

Genesis 12:1–4

The LORD had said to Abram, "Go from your country, your people and your father's household to the land I will show you.

"I will make you into a great nation,
and I will bless you;
I will make your name great,
and you will be a blessing.
I will bless those who bless you,
and whoever curses you I will curse;
and all peoples on earth
will be blessed through you."

> So Abram went, as the LORD had told him; and
> Lot went with him. Abram was seventy-five years
> old when he set out from Harran.

1. How do we know that Abraham trusted God's promise
   when he heard it? How do we know if he continued to
   trust this promise?

2. What does it look like for God to keep this covenant?
   What might it mean for this covenant to shape someone's
   life today?

Teachers of the church from Saint Augustine to the present have emphasized how faith is rooted in God's promise, not our own. We make promises not because we know that we can keep them, but because we know we have been claimed by a God who is faithful. Consider together this passage from the eighteenth-century evangelist John Wesley:

> Yea, the very same words, considered in different respects, are parts both of the law and of the gospel: If they are considered as commandments, they are parts of the law; if as promises, of the gospel. Thus, "Thou shalt love the Lord thy God with all thy heart," when considered as a commandment, is a branch of the law; when regarded as a promise, is an essential part of the gospel—the gospel being no other than the commands of the law, proposed by way of promise.

3. Have you experienced religion that was only command? How does it change your perception of faith if it is "proposed by way of promise"?

4. What difference does this deep sense of grace seem to make in the life of someone like Jean Vanier?

Living the Life

1. How does the idea of covenant make you reconsider your own commitments?

2. Is there a promise that you want to formalize in your life? What sign might both share your commitment with others and point toward your dependence on God?

Ideas for putting faith into practice ...

- Plan a service to "remember your baptism" at your church. Take time to celebrate God's faithfulness and the ways covenant has made your life possible.

- Write a letter to someone you know you've let down. Be honest about your failure to keep your promises. Ask for forgiveness, and share the hope you've found in God's mercy.

- Get together with a group of friends and commit to one another for a year. Formalize the commitment with a service, plan a time to reflect at the end of the year, and talk about practices of confession and reconciliation that will ground your commitment in God's covenant.

Why It Matters Where We Live

Living the Question

Faith in our culture is often portrayed as "spiritual." It's not so much about particular people and places as it is about universal truths and experiences. But our faith is inevitably shaped by particulars like parents and schools, friendships and losses. All of this happens somewhere in particular.

1. What places have shaped your understanding of faith? How do you think about the faith tradition you've inherited—as gift, antique, clutter, skeleton-in-the-closet?

2. Celtic spirituality has a notion of the "thin space" as a place where the divide between heaven and earth is somehow easier to overcome. Are there places that you consider holy ground in your life?

DVD Viewing

Watch the "Why It Matters Where We Live" session from the DVD.

Listening to Lived Theology

1. How is Ann Atwater and C. P. Ellis's unlikely friendship rooted in the history and present-day realities of the South? How does it interrupt normal assumptions about life in that place?

2. Ann Atwater says, "God gave me the gift to reach out and touch." How is her vocation connected to this gift? What does it take to be about to "reach out and touch" in the place where you live?

    I think God wants me to go a little bit further than just praying for people. I think he wants me to absolutely, I call it, "put hands on them." What I mean by "put hands on" is to make sure that the door will be open to that person. —ANN ATWATER

3. In this section Jonathan reflects on the way God's glory is revealed when Jesus forgives Judas. How is this kind of forgiveness evident in Ann's life? What might it look like in the place where you live?

What Jesus shows us is that the glory of God is revealed in human flesh when he's willing to lay his life down for Judas. That's what John's gospel proclaims as the sign that Jesus is God. And when Jesus is raised from the dead and we're invited to be part of Christ's body, that's an invitation to be part of God's movement in this particular way.... We're trying to become the sort of person who can forgive even a friend who betrays us.
—JONATHAN WILSON-HARTGROVE

Listening to Scripture and Tradition

If we pay attention to the story of Scripture, place matters to God's people. Read the following story from John's gospel together, paying attention to the ways Jesus negotiates the differences between himself and the Samaritan woman. Note how these differences are rooted in place:

John 4:1–26

Now Jesus learned that the Pharisees had heard that he was gaining and baptizing more disciples than John — although in fact it was not Jesus who baptized, but his disciples. So he left Judea and went back once more to Galilee.

Now he had to go through Samaria. So he came to a town in Samaria called Sychar, near the plot of ground Jacob had given to his son Joseph. Jacob's well was there, and Jesus, tired as he was from the journey, sat down by the well. It was about noon.

When a Samaritan woman came to draw water, Jesus said to her, "Will you give me a drink?" (His disciples had gone into the town to buy food.)

The Samaritan woman said to him, "You are a Jew and I am a Samaritan woman. How can you ask me for a drink?" (For Jews do not associate with Samaritans.)

Jesus answered her, "If you knew the gift of God and who it is that asks you for a drink, you would have asked him and he would have given you living water."

"Sir," the woman said, "you have nothing to draw with and the well is deep. Where can you get this living water? Are you greater than our father Jacob, who gave us the well and drank from it himself, as did also his sons and his livestock?"

Jesus answered, "Everyone who drinks this water will be thirsty again, but whoever drinks the water I give them will never thirst. Indeed, the water I give them will become in them a spring of water welling up to eternal life."

The woman said to him, "Sir, give me this water so that I won't get thirsty and have to keep coming here to draw water."

He told her, "Go, call your husband and come back."

"I have no husband," she replied.

Jesus said to her, "You are right when you say you have no husband. The fact is, you have had five husbands, and the man you now have is not your husband. What you have just said is quite true."

"Sir," the woman said, "I can see that you are a prophet. Our ancestors worshiped on this mountain, but you Jews claim that the place where we must worship is in Jerusalem."

"Woman," Jesus replied, "believe me, a time is coming when you will worship the Father neither on this mountain nor in Jerusalem. You Samaritans worship what you do not know; we worship what we do know, for salvation is from the Jews. Yet a time is coming and has now come when the true worshipers will worship the Father in the Spirit and in truth, for they are the kind of worshipers the Father seeks. God is spirit, and his worshipers must worship in the Spirit and in truth."

The woman said, "I know that Messiah" (called Christ) "is coming. When he comes, he will explain everything to us."

Then Jesus declared, "I, the one speaking to you —I am he."

1. Jesus and the Samaritan are both aware of Samaria as a place in this story. How does the history of the place shape their relationship? Why does Jesus choose to pass through Samaria rather than go around it?

2. What does Jesus' claim to be Messiah mean for Samaria? What does it mean for those who worship at Jerusalem?

3. What does true worship "in the Spirit and in truth" look like in Samaria? What does it look like where you live?

Chapter 5 in *The Awakening of Hope* highlights the monastic tradition in the history of Christianity as an example of how "true worship" is a combination of prayer and work that encompasses all of life. Faith is not only about what people do in houses of worship or during prayer times. It's about how we live our whole life. It's about how we engage the places where we live. Read the following excerpt from Saint Benedict's *Rule* together:

You should not live the same way other people do; for you, the love of Christ takes first place. You don't lash out in anger or nurse a grudge against some-one who's wronged you (no, you've learned a bet-ter way to deal with the trials that everyone faces). Don't fool yourself. When you greet someone with the peace of Christ, mean it! Don't avoid someone who needs to receive God's love through you. Make promises you can keep, always telling the truth to yourself even as you're honest with others.

Don't fight like other people fight, returning evil for evil (1 Thessalonians 5:15a). Instead, suffer patiently, refusing to pass another's violence on to someone else. Love your enemies (Matthew 5:44). If someone cusses you out, don't strike back with your own assault of words. Find a way to bless them instead. Endure persecution for the sake of justice (cf. Matthew 5:10).

Don't be addicted to your own self-image or to anything else that promises cheap fulfillment or an easy escape from problems. Beware of too much eating or too much sleeping. Watch out for laziness (Romans 12:11a). Don't spend your time complain-ing or talking bad about other people.

Put your hope in God alone. If you notice yourself doing good (that is the point, after all), give God all the credit. You're not doing it on your own. But you can be sure of this: whatever bad habits you hold onto, you get all the credit for those. It's up to you to acknowledge them and make amends.

If you're honest with yourself, you'll tremble at the thought of meeting God face-to-face and shudder when you consider God's judgment. Let that holy fear stir up your desire for living that life that's really life. Never forget: you are going to die. Every single thing you do is infinitely important, because God sees every act, no matter where you are. The moment you have a bad thought, dash it against Christ (he is a solid rock) and confess it to your spiritual director. Don't let a lie or a mean word cross your lips, but speak carefully, avoiding useless talk and the sort of jokes that stir up the worst in people.

Here's what you should do with every spare moment you have: listen to the wisdom of those who've gone before you and devote yourself to prayer. Take time to confess your sins to God every day — not just naming them, but taking time to grieve the great harm they've done to you and the whole universe. In your tears resolve to leave your addictions and protective mechanisms behind.

Don't give in to your twisted desires (Galatians 5:16b) despise that voice that whispers, "Do what you need to do." Listen instead to the leadership of your community even if their actions (God forbid) don't match up with their advice. Remember what our Lord said about the Pharisees: Do what they say, not what they do (Matthew 23:3a).

There's no sense acting like you've achieved sainthood. Instead, work on becoming a saint in every little thing you do so your actions might one day speak for themselves. Make God's good words your constant guide: treasure chastity; don't harbor hatred or jealousy; and don't let envy drive a single action. Don't get into arguing, and turn your back on arrogance. Respect the wise and love the inexperienced in community. Out of love for Christ, say a prayer for the one who's become your enemy. If you have an argument with someone during the day, make peace with him before the sun goes down.

Last of all; never lose hope in God's mercy.

These are the tools of the spiritual craft that I want to pass on to you as a master carpenter passes his toolbox on to an apprentice. If we use them day and night, never laying them aside or getting distracted from our task, then we'll be able to return them to the true Master Carpenter when we meet him face-to-face. Our wages will be the reward he has promised: What the eye has not seen nor the ear heard ... God has prepared for those who love him (1 Corinthians 2:9).

The workshop where we put all these tools to constant use is the community where God has called us to stay put.

4. What on this list do you typically think of as part of your "spiritual life"? Are any of these "tools" surprising?

5. Why is the workshop where these tools are put to use the "community where God has called us to stay put"? What is the significance of a particular place for these practices?

Living the Life

1. Does the conviction that God took on flesh and lived among us change the way you think about how you live in the place where you are? What, if anything, does it change?

2. What kind of practices and rhythms might make "true worship" more doable in your life?

3. Who are the Ann Atwaters in your community? How can you learn from elders who have lived faithfully in the place where you are?

Ideas for putting faith into practice ...

- Make a map of the neighborhood or streets that are walkable from your home. Write the names of people you know in their houses or places of business. Pray for these people. Try to fill in the blanks for people you don't know.

- Research a local saint. Learn her story and tell others how her faithfulness has shaped the place where you live.

- Join a committee or board that is working on something that will affect people where you live after you are gone.

Why We Live Together

Living the Question

If we pay attention to our deepest longings, all of us want to know what group we belong to and where we can be our true selves. We need community. And yet, at the same time, we resist it. We hide from those close to us, we resent family expectations, we try to protect ourselves from the pain that relationship with others can bring.

1. Do you think of yourself as an introvert or an extrovert? How does your personality shape the way you interact with groups of people?

2. What experiences have shaped your understanding of community? What have you seen that you want more of? What do you want to avoid?

DVD Viewing

Watch the "Why We Live Together" session from the DVD.

Listening to Lived Theology

1. Jonathan likes to talk about church as "God's counterculture in the world." What patterns and practices of community life interrupt the habits of our world's broken systems? How does a community both practice a radical alternative and acknowledge its own frailty and brokenness? Jonathan wrote, "We live this radical way of Jesus not as people who are perfect, but as people who know the story." How does God's story shape a community?

> *Independence is not a gospel value; it's an American value. The gospel teaches us interdependence. It teaches us community. Part of the good news is that we're not alone in the world.*
> —SHANE CLAIBORNE

2. Shane talks about an "intentional village" where he and neighbors are trying to live the gospel at dinner tables and in living rooms. How might you invest in the fabric of your neighborhood with others? How could this day-to-day form of church connect with local congregations?

3. What structures help community to thrive? What rhythms of your life lead you into deeper relationship with others and with God?

Listening to Scripture and Tradition

In chapter 6, Jonathan notes how the New Testament teaching about the fellowship of those who gather in Jesus' name is closely connected to the presence of God's Spirit among them. Read together the following prayer from Paul's letter to the Ephesians:

Ephesians 1:15–23

For this reason, ever since I heard about your faith in the Lord Jesus and your love for all God's people, I have not stopped giving thanks for you, remembering you in my prayers. I keep asking that the God of our Lord Jesus Christ, the glorious Father, may give you the Spirit of wisdom and revelation, so that you may know him better. I pray that the eyes of your heart may be enlightened in order that you may know the hope to which he has called you, the riches of his glorious inheritance in his holy people, and his incomparably great power for us who believe. That power is the same as the mighty strength he exerted when he raised Christ from the dead and seated him at his right hand in the heavenly realms, far above all rule and authority, power and dominion, and every name that is invoked, not only in the present age but also in the one to come. And God placed all things under his feet and appointed him to be head over everything for the church, which is his body, the fullness of him who fills everything in every way.

1. What does it mean when Paul writes to those gathered at Ephesus about the riches of their inheritance in God's "holy people." What does this inheritance give them access to? Are those same riches available to us?

2. Why is the power that raised Christ from the dead so important for this community in Ephesus? What role does the Spirit play in their understanding of this power?

3. In the ancient world, to put something or someone "under the feet" of another symbolized care and protection (they were not there to be trampled upon, but rather sheltered). What does it mean that God has placed "all things" under Christ's feet "for the church"? In what way are people called together in Jesus' name a blessing to the place where you live?

The father of Reformed theology, John Calvin, summarized Christian teaching about community by saying what Saint Augustine before him had said: the church is our Mother. Consider his words together:

> For those to whom [God] is Father the church may also be Mother.... For there is no other way to enter into life unless this mother conceive us in her womb, give us birth, nourish us at her breast, and lastly, unless she keep us under her care and guidance until, putting off mortal flesh, we become like angels. Our weakness does not allow us to be dismissed from her school until we have been pupils all our lives. Furthermore, away from her bosom one cannot hope for any forgiveness of sins or any salvation.

4. What does the image of "mother" suggest about our need for shared life with a community of faith?

5. Why does Calvin think that we cannot be saved or forgiven without a community called church?

Living the Life

1. How has this session helped you think about the community you're already part of? How might you be called to grow in your relationships or in your commitment to a particular group?

2. Is there a particular way that you can imagine growing closer to God by drawing closer to a community of people?

3. What structures or practices might help you and others in your life to grow closer as a community in Jesus' name?

Ideas for putting faith into practice ...

- Pool some money with a group of friends for a year. Meet once a week to pray together and discuss how you can invest your resources in God's work.

- Plan to eat with the same people twice a week for three months. Take a retreat together at the end of the three months to talk about what you're learning.

- Find out if anyone in your church has friends or family in prison. Ask whether that person might want to come home to your house when he is released.

Why We Would Rather Die Than Kill

Living the Question

Even though we often only think about it in the "hard cases," when we're facing a difficult decision, faith shapes how we engage the world and respond to other people. People don't always agree on what is right and wrong in a particular situation. But we try to figure these things out based on the convictions we hold dear and the story we believe about how the world exists and why.

1. Have you ever had an experience where you were surprised to find that you were convicted that something was the "right" thing to do? Share about that experience.

2. Have you ever had a conviction that led you to live differently than those around you? How did that feel? What sustained you in that decision?

DVD Viewing

Watch the "Why We Would Rather Die Than Kill" session from the DVD.

Listening to Lived Theology

1. Dayna says, "Ethan's life was and is a gift from God ... no less beautiful and joyful than any other child's life. And also, because his life was and is a good gift, his death was terrible, horrible, painful beyond what you can say in words." What gifts does Dayna point to in her own life that made it possible for her to both embrace and grieve her son?

> *In the kingdom of God, things don't always end up happy. But they can still be beautiful.*
> —SAM WELLS

2. Shane asks, "If every person is made in the image of God, how does that impact the way we think about the death penalty, poverty, militarism, and war?" Where do you find it most difficult to live a "consistent ethic of life"?

3. Shane says, "We should be the hardest people in the world to convince that violence is necessary." But he also acknowledges that Christians have often been quick to judge and condemn their neighbors. Why do you think Jesus' radical love is so difficult to practice?

> *One of the things I love about Jesus is how you get this sense that he is interrupting death everywhere it raises its ugly face, and that he's about life and dignity, and that no person—no matter how deeply wounded or stepped on they are—no person is beyond redemption.*
> —SHANE CLAIBORNE

Listening to Scripture and Tradition

The way of life that interrupts violence with love is a way we learn from Jesus. But it's also a way of living that we have to practice, because the patterns of violence are deep in each of us. Read together the following outline from Matthew's gospel for how a community should deal with the ways people hurt one another.

Matthew 18:15–18

"If your brother or sister sins, go and point out their fault, just between the two of you. If they listen to you, you have won them over. But if they will not listen, take one or two others along, so that 'every matter may be established by the testimony of two or three witnesses.' If they still refuse to listen, tell it to the church; and if they refuse to listen even to the church, treat them as you would a pagan or a tax collector.

"Truly I tell you, whatever you bind on earth will be bound in heaven, and whatever you loose on earth will be loosed in heaven."

1. Why is pointing out someone else's faults an important part of learning to love well?

2. How does this process encourage us to practice a life of consistent love? What habits does it encourage in people who take it seriously?

3. How did Jesus treat "pagans and tax collectors"? What does this suggest about how we love when the process "doesn't work"?

Consider together this description of the early church from the Letter to Diognetus.

> The Christians are distinguished from other men neither by country, nor by language, nor by the customs that they observe; for they neither inhabit cities of their own, nor employ a peculiar form of speech. They dwell in their own countries, but simply as sojourners. They marry, as do all others; they beget children; but they do not destroy their offspring. They have a common table, but not a common bed. They are in the flesh, but they do not live after the flesh. They pass their days on earth, but they are citizens of heaven. They obey the prescribed laws, and at the same time surpass the laws by their lives. They love all men, and are persecuted by all. They are unknown and condemned; they are put to death, and restored to life. They are poor, yet they make many rich; they are lacking all things, and yet abound in all; they are dishonored, and yet in their very dishonor are glorified. They are spoken of as evil, and yet are justified; they are reviled, and bless; they are insulted and repay the insult with honor; they do good, yet are punished as evildoers.

4. What about the early Christians' way of life was noteworthy to this observer? Do you see parallels to this way of life in our world today?

5. How is faith in Jesus reflected in the way of life that is described here?

6. What would you guess these Christians believed about the world they lived in and the people who were their neighbors?

Living the Life

1. How does the way you live reflect what you believe? Are there ways you can see that your life betrays a lack of trust in the things you say you believe?

2. How might you practice day-to-day the kind of love that makes it possible to forgive an enemy?

3. Where do you feel challenged to "choose life" this week? What might it look like for you to practice a consistent ethic of life where you are?

Ideas for putting faith into practice ...

- Write to someone on death row. Listen to their story and ask God to help you see what it means to trust that no one is beyond redemption.

- Try to talk honestly with a friend who has offended you. Tell them that you forgive them. Put Matthew 18 into practice as training in the truth-telling that makes peace possible.

- Ask who are the "invisible" people in your community. Make a special effort to get to know them this week.

Why We Share Good News

Living the Question

Most people like to share the things that excite them with people they love. Sometimes, if we're overcome with delight, we might even share some good news with a complete stranger. But sharing about faith, however sincere, can easily seem "preachy." One person's good news can sound like bad news to someone else.

1. Have you ever had some news you were so excited about that you had to tell someone?

2. Have you had an experience of feeling hustled by people who wanted to share their faith with you?

DVD Viewing

Watch the "Why We Share Good News" session from the DVD.

Listening to Lived Theology

1. Shane says, "The gospel spreads best not through force but through fascination." How has Christ's good news fascinated you or someone you know? Is the Christianity you've seen practiced fascinating? Why or why not?

> God so loved the world that he didn't just send a little flyer, he sent his own son. It's that personal love that has caught the world's attention for hundreds of years.
> —SHANE CLAIBORNE

2. Reverend Barber says, "I don't know a salvation apart from social justice.... There's no way to have a crisis conversion of the spirit and not be engaged in an argument with the world." How have you seen spiritual conversion connected with a new way of engaging the world? What do "God's politics" have to do with evangelism?

> I don't know any way to talk about Christianity and not be concerned about injustice. I think it's an abdication of my Christian responsibility not to remind politicians that the budget you pass in these legislatures is a moral document. You can't serve God and Mammon.
> —REVEREND BARBER

3. How has the gospel story claimed Reverend Barber's life? He says, "I hope that when I die those who remain will be able to say that I tried to be part of the community that kept believing in love … and that we held true to the gospel plow." What does it mean that his hope for his own life is a hope for a "we"? When you think about your own life, is there a "we" that your hope is tied to?

Listening to Scripture and Tradition

Christians share good news neither to show our neighbors why Christianity is "right" nor to save people from other religions, but to name the story that helps us tell the truth about ourselves and our world. Because we trust this story to be true, we believe it is "true for everyone." To the extent that the broken systems of this world resist God's truth, evangelism is a confrontation with the principalities and powers.

Read the following account of some early Christians' confrontation with the powers of their day.

Acts 4:5–20

The next day the rulers, the elders and the teachers of the law met in Jerusalem. Annas the high priest was there, and so were Caiaphas, John, Alexander and others of the high priest's family. They had Peter and John brought before them and began to question them: "By what power or what name did you do this?"

Then Peter, filled with the Holy Spirit, said to them: "Rulers and elders of the people! If we are being called to account today for an act of kindness shown to a man who was lame and are being asked how he was healed, then know this, you and all the people of Israel: It is by the name of Jesus Christ of Nazareth, whom you crucified but whom God raised from the dead, that this man stands before you healed. Jesus is

" 'the stone you builders rejected,
    which has become the cornerstone.'

"Salvation is found in no one else, for there is no other name under heaven given to mankind by which we must be saved."

When they saw the courage of Peter and John and realized that they were unschooled, ordinary men, they were astonished and they took note that these men had been with Jesus. But since they could see the man who had been healed standing there with them, there was nothing they could say. So they ordered them to withdraw from the Sanhedrin and then conferred together. "What are we going to do with these men?" they asked. "Everyone living in Jerusalem knows they have performed a notable sign, and we cannot deny it. But to stop this thing from spreading any further among the people, we must warn them to speak no longer to anyone in this name."

Then they called them in again and commanded them not to speak or teach at all in the name of Jesus. But Peter and John replied, "Which is right in God's eyes: to listen to you, or to him? You be the judges! As for us, we cannot help speaking about what we have seen and heard."

1. What signs gave power to the words Peter and John spoke about Jesus? Have you witnessed the power of healing among people who have "been with Jesus"?

2. Why were the authorities threatened by the actions and words of these early evangelists? How did their message threaten the broken systems of power and control?

3. Some Christians quote "no other name" from this passage to suggest that the truth of Christianity excludes the truths of other faith traditions. But Peter and John are not holding the name of Jesus up against the name of Buddha or Allah. They are saying that the One whom their leaders have rejected is the only One who can save. How does the truth that Peter and John testify to engage the truth of other stories? Have you experienced faithful Christian witness that also honors the truth in other traditions? Are there ways that other faith traditions have helped you understand the truth of Christianity?

Living the Life

1. Is there a new way of sharing the good news that you've been able to imagine through this study? What might that look like for you this week?

2. If you invite someone to trust in Jesus, what else are you inviting them into? How does your understanding of evangelism connect to your understanding of community and ethics?

Ideas for putting faith into practice ...

- Ask a neighbor or coworker who is not Christian what they think of Christianity. Have a conversation about how your understanding of faith is the same and how it's different.

- Spend some time getting to know another faith tradition. Visit a mosque or a temple. Ask someone there to explain to you their understanding of the world. Ask yourself if there are ways their tradition might help you see the truth of Christianity more clearly.

- Practice explaining why your life would not make sense if the gospel were not true.

Acknowledgments

THE IDEA FOR THIS PROJECT GREW OUT OF YEARS OF WORKing on a project called *Common Prayer: A Liturgy For Ordinary Radicals* (commonprayer.net). As I witnessed the power of an ancient practice like liturgy to help us pray and sing the hope of God's movement in our time, I was inspired to dust off some other ancient practices of the church. Catechism cried out, and dozens of friends who serve as pastors helped me listen carefully to the kinds of questions people are asking in their congregations. I'm also deeply grateful for my work with the School for Conversion (newmonasticism.org) that has allowed me to listen in on the questions people have asked of new monastic communities over the past decade.

Since Jesus said the kingdom of God is always about bringing together "some things old and some things new" (Matthew 13:52, paraphrased), Shane Claiborne and I decided to partner with some of the friends who inspire hope in our lives to create a video resource as part of this contemporary catechism. I don't know who I'd be without the friendship of Shane, Chris Haw, Jean Vanier, Ann Atwater, Dayna Olson-Getty, and William Barber. I'm so grateful for their lives, and glad for their willingness to let us share parts of their stories on the DVD. We hope the new technology only enhances the lived theology and ancient wisdom. Shane and I are both grateful for our friend, Travis Reed, with the Work of the People (theworkofthepeople.org) who's committed to not only telling good stories, but to using video to create "visual liturgy."

In the modern world, teachers of the church do not only find themselves in churches and communities, but also in colleges and universities. Though I'm not myself an academic, I recognize the great gift of people who dedicate themselves to learning and "sounding down" the wisdom of the ages. Thankfully, some of these people are also generous friends. Thanks especially to the following who served as a theological advisory board for this project: Jason Byassee, Gerald Schlabach, Bill Cavanaugh, Kelly Johnson, Stanley Hauerwas, Dorothy Bass, Charles Marsh, Margaret Kim Peterson, and Jonathan Wilson.

Working on this catechism project has helped me to name not only the importance of lived theology in saints and communities that we see and touch, but also the importance of those friends with whom we make sense of our experiences in conversation. Since I was in junior high school, Marty Bywaters-Baldwin has been my constant companion on the journey toward making sense of what God is up to in our lives and in our world. Because we hashed all of this and more out on basketball courts and running trails, in letters sent halfway around the world and in those quiet hours after the kids had gone to bed, this book is dedicated to him.

Notes

1. From General William Booth's famous "I'll Fight" speech, which was given at his final public appearance (Royal Albert Hall, London, 1912). Although Booth himself never wrote out these words, they were published in 1927, and various people who were present at Booth's speech confirmed that he actually spoke these words.

2. Columba Stewart, "The Origins and Fate of Monasticism," *Spiritus* 10 (2010), 257.

3. Wendell Berry, "In Distrust of Movements," *The Sun* 297 (September 2000).

4. Daniel Hillel, *Out of the Earth: Civilization and the Life of Soil* (London: Aurum Press, 1991), 23.

5. Norman Wirzba, *Food and Faith: A Theology of Eating* (Cambridge, UK: Cambridge University Press, 2011), 178.

6. For a good edition of this, see *The Rule of Saint Benedict* (New York: Vintage, 1998).

7. Henry L. Carrigan, ed., *The Wisdom of the Desert Fathers and Mothers* (Orleans, Mass.: Paraclete, 2010).

8. Saint John Climacus, *The Ladder of Divine Ascent* (Elwood City, Penn.: Holy Transfiguration Monastery, 2001), 195.

9. Margaret McKenna, in *School(s) for Conversion: 12 Marks of a New Monasticism*, Rutba House, eds., (Eugene, Ore: Cascade Books, 2005), 25.

10. Story paraphrased from Thomas Merton, *The Wisdom of the Desert* (Boston: Shambhala, 1994).

11. From a hymn by Thomas Shepherd (1665–1739), "Must Jesus Bare the Cross Alone," first published in 1693. This verse is by Shepherd, while other, later writers wrote subsequent verses to this hymn.

12. Brother Lawrence's friends and fellow monks compiled a book of his sayings and their reminiscences of him, called *Practicing the Presence of God*, which is one of the most accessible and beloved volumes of classic Christian literature.

Common Prayer Pocket Edition

A Liturgy for Ordinary Radicals

Shane Claiborne and Jonathan Wilson-Hartgrove

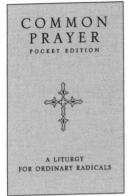

Common Prayer Pocket Edition helps individuals and today's diverse church pray together across traditions and denominations. With an ear to the particulars of various liturgical prayer traditions, and using an advisory team of liturgy experts, the authors have created a tapestry of prayer that celebrates the best of each tradition. This convenient and portable book also includes tools for prayer scattered throughout to aid those unfamiliar with liturgy and deepen the prayer life of those already familiar with liturgical prayer. *Common Prayer Pocket Edition* adds new prayers for compline (late evening) and for individual use, such as prayers for travel, protection, and various blessings. It includes a table of days and readings for the morning prayers as well as an annotated list of saints and days to remember. Churches and individuals who desire a deeper prayer life — and those familiar with Shane Claiborne and New Monasticism — will enjoy the tools offered in this book as a fresh take on liturgy.

Available in stores and online!

God's Economy

Redefining the Health and Wealth Gospel

Jonathan Wilson-Hartgrove

Are you dissatisfied with the gospel of health and wealth?

Health-and-wealth proponents urge Christians to claim material blessings on earth. Others insist that God's best gifts can't be enjoyed until heaven. The truth of God's intentions, writes acclaimed author Jonathan Wilson-Hartgrove, is far greater than either perspective suggests.

With persuasive enthusiasm, Jonathan Wilson-Hartgrove draws from Jesus' teachings on money, exploring five tactics for living in God's economy of abundance. Then, he demonstrates how people have practiced these tactics in the past, as well as what these principles can do for you, your family, and your church today.

From your human relationships to your spiritual life, this practical guide cuts through the clutter and invites you to discover what can happen when you invest in *God's Economy.*

Available in stores and online!

Mirror to the Church

Resurrecting Faith after Genocide in Rwanda

Emmanuel Katongole
with Jonathan Wilson-Hartgrove

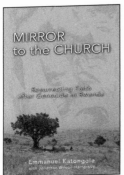

We learn who we are as we walk together in the way of Jesus. So I want to invite you on a pilgrimage.

Rwanda was often held up as a model of evangelization in Africa. Yet in 1994, beginning on the Thursday of Easter week, Christians killed other Christians, often in the same churches where they had worshiped together. The most Christianized country in Africa became the site of its worst genocide. With a mother who was a Hutu and a father who was a Tutsi, author Emmanuel Katongole is uniquely qualified to point out that the tragedy in Rwanda is also a mirror reflecting the deep brokenness of the church in the West. Rwanda brings us to a cry of lament on our knees where together we learn that we must interrupt these patterns of brokenness.

But Rwanda also brings us to a place of hope. Indeed, the only hope for our world after Rwanda's genocide is a new kind of Christian identity for the global body of Christ — a people on pilgrimage together, a mixed group, bearing witness to a new identity made possible by the Gospel.

Share Your Thoughts

With the Author: Your comments will be forwarded to the author when you send them to *zauthor@zondervan.com*.

With Zondervan: Submit your review of this book by writing to *zreview@zondervan.com*.

Free Online Resources at
www.zondervan.com

Zondervan AuthorTracker: Be notified whenever your favorite authors publish new books, go on tour, or post an update about what's happening in their lives at www.zondervan.com/authortracker.

Daily Bible Verses and Devotions: Enrich your life with daily Bible verses or devotions that help you start every morning focused on God. Visit www.zondervan.com/newsletters.

Free Email Publications: Sign up for newsletters on Christian living, academic resources, church ministry, fiction, children's resources, and more. Visit www.zondervan.com/newsletters.

Zondervan Bible Search: Find and compare Bible passages in a variety of translations at www.zondervanbiblesearch.com.

Other Benefits: Register to receive online benefits like coupons and special offers, or to participate in research.

ZONDERVAN.com/
AUTHORTRACKER
follow your favorite authors